FRIGID WOMEN

by

Sue & Victoria Riches

FRIGID WOMEN

by

Sue & Victoria Riches

Editor Gordon Medcalf

Publisher Travellerseye

Frigid Women

1st Edition

Published by Travellerseye Ltd.

Head Office:

    30 St Mary's Street,

    Bridgnorth,

    Shropshire,

    WV16 4DW.

    United Kingdom

    tel: (0044) 1746 766447

    fax: (0044) 1746 766665

    e-mail books@travellerseye.com

Published October 1998.

Set in Times

Cover design Micky Hiscocks & Mark Edgington

Printed and bound in Great Britain by Creative Print and Design Wales

iv

Acknowledgements

Caroline Hamilton - For having a dream to walk to the North Pole.

Pen Hadow - He made Caroline's dream a reality.

Matty McNair and Denise Martin - The unsung heroines of the expedition. Without them we would never have got there.

Geoff Somers - Who taught us to survive in the Arctic

Our Sponsors:

McVitie's Penguin Biscuits

Angela Mortimer plc

Bradstock Insurance Broking Group

Canadian Airlines

Carrington's Performance Fabrics

Damart Thermawear

Neutrogena Norwegian Formula

Vander Waterproofs

To all those at Resolute, especially Gary and Diane Guy who made us so welcome.

An enormous thank you to all our friends and family. Without their support and encouragement we may well have been left behind!

And finally, Bindon Plowman - Who gave us the title of the book!

A word from the publisher in support of 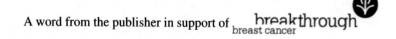 breakthrough breast cancer

Anyone who suffers from cancer will have their lives changed forever - regardless of the outcome. Sue Riches (one of the authors of this book) was diagnosed as having breast cancer, which resulted in a mastectomy. This gave Sue a new perspective on life and contributed to her decision to apply to join the expedition to the North Pole.

She has been able to lead a happy fulfilling life since the operation, but is only too aware that from the 1 in 12 women who will suffer from the disease at some point in their lifetime, over 1,000 die each month.

As a result of her experience, Sue feels able to support those who are in any way affected by the disease. 10 pence from the sale of each copy of this book will go to Breakthrough Breast Cancer, a registered charity. For further details about Breakthrough read their Chief Executive's letter on page 229.

Contents

		Page
Foreword by Dawn French		ix-x

Part One   **"Adventurers Sought ..."**

Chapter One	The Reasons Why	1-16
Chapter Two	Survival of the Fittest	17-42
Chapter Three	Media, Money & Muscles	43-66
Chapter Four	Resolute Bay	67-90
Chapter Five	The Ice Mice	91-116

Part Two   **"Penguin Charlie"**

Chapter Six	Diaries: Stepping Out	119-140
Chapter Seven	Diaries: Stepping In	141-170
Chapter Eight	Diaries: Find Your Own Runway	171-190
Chapter Nine	Happy Landings and Sad Partings	191-210
Chapter Ten	The Pole and After	211-227
Postscript	The Way is North	228-229

Appendices		230-239

Foreword

A relay expedition to the North Pole? Discomfort, pain and cold? - No thanks. I am one of the 99.9% of women who, faced with this sort of prospect, makes another cup of hot chocolate and settles down in front of the telly as a sort of slothful protest. I can't think of a much worse scenario than joining this adventure. HOWEVER, I am also someone who *wishes* that I *did* have the courage, determination and sheer bloody mindedness to leap at an opportunity like this ....

Imagine how utterly delighted I was, then, to meet up with Caroline Hamilton who wanted me to be the Patron-come-Mascot for the whole shebang, thereby giving me the chance to go on the expedition vicariously through these remarkable women. I pledged my support there and then, since it was impossible to resist Caroline Hamilton's irrepressible spirit, and I vowed to make it my duty to satisfy the men folk whilst they were away. (To this day none of the men folk have taken advantage of this offer which, let me tell you, was a huge disappointment!)

At the beginning I thought it was going to be a cinch. Nothing much was required of me, except to jolly some people along and encourage a few sponsors to invest at a big launch party. Not a problem.

However, once the expedition started I was kept in touch with the progress of all the teams, via the Internet, faxes and phone calls. I found myself getting more involved and more worried as the fascinating tales of mishaps, weather problems, victories and failures revealed themselves. I was on the edge on my seat, especially since most of the information was virtually incomprehensible to an ice-virgin like me, and I always feared the worst. As each team reached its goal, another hurdle was conquered and I rested *slightly* easier! Imagine the joy and relief when the final team, Echo, made it safely and stood on the very top of the world in all their girlie glory! What a huge, collaborative triumph. I leapt about my house like a mad thing and celebrated with much chocolate and shouting.

I went to meet Echo as they arrived back on the tarmac at Heathrow and believe me, I never want to smell anything like them again. I mean I love them, but boy they were high!

This book, lovingly written by Sue & Victoria Riches is an account of their wonderful experience and their vital contribution to this historic and remarkable journey. A journey that they went on physically, mentally and spiritually; inside and out. I am so proud to have been associated with them.

This story is a fantastic celebration of adventure, courage, friendship and love. Enjoy it all you would be adventurers ....And dream on!

Dawn French.

We would like to dedicate this book to

Jeremy / Dad Philip and Edward.

Without their support we could not have done it.

Part One

Adventurers Sought

"The ice was here, the ice was there,

The ice was all around:

It crack'd and growl'd, and roar'd and howl'd

Like noises in a swound!"

From *The Rime of the Ancient Mariner*

Samuel Taylor Coleridge (1772-1834)

THE
ARCTIC
REGION

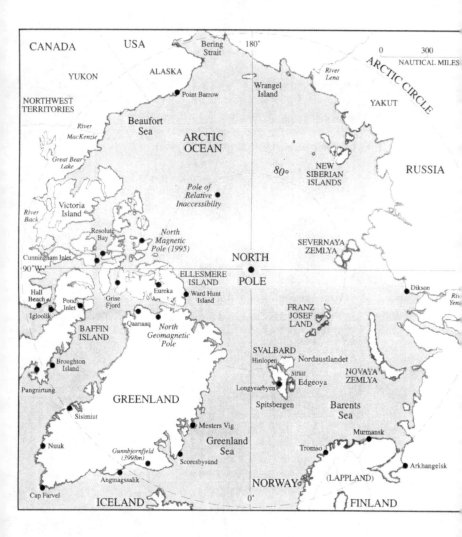

Chapter One

The Reasons Why

Sue:

I crawled through the tent doorway at midnight, in full sunlight, the shadows long, the ice crystals shimmering in the air, a stunning view in front of me, and wearing just a set of Damart thermal underwear, a pair of socks and my water bottle insulators as slippers and I wondered to myself, is this the Arctic as I had imagined it? Why was I even going through the door at this time of night? There are no loos in the Arctic.

Was it really as Apsley Cherry-Garrard described it in his book, *The Worst Journey In The World:* "Polar exploration is at once the cleanest and most isolated way of having a bad time which has been devised" - enough to put anyone off!

Why did I want to go there? I have never had the burning desire to see the polar wastes since the age of six, or wanted to pull a sledge over rough sea ice that is likely to split open in front of you, or indeed to revel in temperatures of -40°C or less. I like my comforts, my electric blanket, warm fires and delicious food, so why go to the Arctic Ocean for a six week holiday on ice?

For the answers to these questions we have to go back nearly two years ......

*

Victoria:

August 1995. Mid summer in London. The tube was packed with workers and tourists all on their way somewhere and all in their own little world. As usual I was reading the paper, hanging onto the handrails

1

and trying to avoid various smelly armpits all at the same time. Why was I here? I loved my job as a recruitment consultant for Angela Mortimer plc, but hated living in London. There must be more to life than this. Having come to the normal conclusion that I could not think of an alternative career which did not involve commuting, I went back to reading my paper.

Then I saw it:

"Adventurers are being sought for the first attempt by an all woman team to walk to the North Pole."

For some reason this opening line caught my eye. This must have been fate; here was my alternative to commuting. I read on:

"Prospective candidates will have to pass an SAS based selection test before they will get anywhere near putting on a pair of ice boots. Applications are invited from women of any age, background and occupation, but they will have to prove fitness and commitment. They will have to put up with real pain and discomfort. They will wonder every ten steps what they are doing but they have the opportunity to take part in an epic endeavour." It sounds corny but at that moment I knew that this was what I wanted to do, I felt on an absolute high.

I got to the office and tested various people's reactions. The normal comment was:

"Are you crazy, stupid or just insane?" But I knew that I could do it and that this was to be a turning point in my life. Having spoken to the team members since, we all felt that same rush of adrenalin when we first heard or read about the expedition. As Geoff Somers, our trainer up at Resolute Bay, was to say to us:

"If someone asks you why you are doing it, they will never

understand."

As always that evening I rang Mum up for a chat and just in passing mentioned that I had seen an article in the *Daily Telegraph* and was thinking of applying to go on an expedition to the North Pole. Most mothers would probably have said "Yes dear," and carried on with the conversation, however Mum is not most Mothers. To this day we dispute what happened next, I say that Mum invited herself, and Mum says that I asked her along. The fact remains that Mum also applied to go on the expedition.

So what was this expedition, who was organising it and what was the aim? It all started in June 1995. Caroline Hamilton, a film financier, had an ambition to stand on the top of the world. This dream originated when she sat at the edge of the Arctic Circle in Iceland watching the sun dip to the horizon at midnight and rise again a few minutes later. She had travelled extensively throughout the world and this one ambition eluded her, until she heard about the Polar Travel Company, a specialist travel and guide service for the polar regions headed up by Pen Hadow. Caroline asked Pen if she could make a journey 'the explorer's way' to the North Pole - on foot, but she wanted to make the journey within her normal holiday leave, her budget should not exceed £1,500 and any preparation should be in her free time.

The solution was surprisingly simple and completely original - a relay from Ward Hunt Island to the Pole. There would be five teams of four people (Alpha, Bravo, Charlie, Delta and Echo), and each team would train for one week at Resolute Bay in the North West Territories in Canada before being flown onto the ice to relieve the previous team and continue North. Two female guides would accompany the expedition the whole

3

way and in doing so would become the first women in the world to walk to the North Pole. Two women had been to the Pole before, Bancroft (USA) and Mako (Japan), but in larger expeditions with the assistance of dogs or snowmobiles, i.e. we would be the first ever female, human - powered expedition.

Suddenly everyone was asking me questions. Where is Ward Hunt Island? What is the difference between the Geographic and Magnetic North Poles? What wildlife will you see up there? As I realised I had not a clue about where I was intending to go a serious amount of reading followed, and before long I could answer all the basic questions. There are in fact six 'poles', three in the Arctic and three in the Antarctic. The Geographic Pole is the one at the top/bottom of the world, i.e. where the axes of the world are, and the ones that most explorers aim to reach. In the case of the North Pole it is on frozen sea ice and although its position remains constant there is no actual pole as the ice is always moving. The South Pole is static, on land, and a permanent base marks the spot. The Magnetic Poles are where a compass points to and in the case of the Magnetic North Pole is actually approximately six hundred miles away, to the South West of the Geographic North Pole. In other words, when you want to walk to the Geographic North Pole your compass needs to read 91^0E - very confusing. A similar discrepancy applies in the south, but the Magnetic South Pole is in fact in the sea. There are also Geomagnetic North and South Poles - rarely seen as a destination by polar explorers.

For an expedition to the Geographic North Pole, there are two main places to set out from, Canada or Siberia. We chose to set out from Canada. The northernmost tip is called Ward Hunt Island, a tiny outcrop

4

off Ellesmere Island, just under five hundred nautical miles from the North Pole. The nearest community is on Cornwallis Island some five hundred odd miles away, so that is where all training takes place, and where 'base camp' is set up for most expeditions. This small community was a place with which we were going to become very familiar, Resolute Bay, almost one thousand miles from the Pole. North of Resolute there is very little sign of human habitation. The Polaris mines are a short distance away and on Ellesmere Island there is Eureka, a weather station that is manned throughout the year by a hardy band of eight men, who tend to work three months on, one month off. Finally there is Alert, a US military base with very few personnel.

The final area where I had to brush up my knowledge was Arctic wildlife, the big question being polar bears or penguins? I soon learned that polar bears live in the Arctic, along with foxes, hares and various birds (which only really make an appearance in the low Arctic), therefore by a process of elimination penguins live at the South Pole. People always ask if we saw much wildlife and our answer invokes mixed emotions. Apart from the odd husky and two Arctic hares at Resolute we saw nothing.

In some ways this was a blessing as we did not fancy being a polar bear's breakfast. However the Arctic is a paradise for wild animals and it seems such a shame to have gone so far and not seen a thing. This is unfortunately true for most expeditions and the reason is very simple; most animals live in the low Arctic as that is where most of the food is. Once we were on the ice, if we had seen a polar bear as far North as we were, we would have been in trouble as we would have been the only food around for many miles! We did carry a rifle, but polar bears are a protected species and you would only kill one in an absolute emergency.

People always ask me why I wanted to go to the North Pole, as it is a pretty drastic way to change your life. I have spent many hours thinking of a suitable answer and the only one I can come up with is that I was brought up to believe that nothing is impossible. As a child I had a wonderful existence with my holidays spent either at home in the Midlands or in Perthshire on my grandparents' farm. My two brothers and I spent hours just playing outdoors or climbing various hills and mountains. This is where my love of the outdoors stems from. I am not a fanatical walker or climber, but just love the peace and solitude that exists away from the towns and cities.

Along the way I have had various moments when I thought my life was going to fall apart, but Mum and Dad have always had a caring, no nonsense attitude: be positive, things can only get better. This approach has I suppose given me the drive and determination to carry on no matter what. At the age of seventeen life seemed excellent. I was head girl of my school, had various offers for university and for sponsorship while there to read engineering - what could go wrong? I very soon learned: I failed all my A-levels. At the time I thought Mum and Dad would be livid, but not a bit of it, they told me to continue with my GAP year as planned (teaching in Canada), and we could sort out everything when I came back.

As it turned out I had a change of direction whilst in Canada, and when I returned to the UK I took three new A-levels in eight months and went off to Newcastle University to read Politics. All along I had the support and love of my parents telling me that life had not collapsed, to pull myself together and get on with it and it will sort itself out. And sure

6

enough it did!

My friends have always said that I do too much and if anyone was going to the North Pole it would have been me. However I am convinced that anyone can go as long as they believe in themselves. It is hell at times, no doubt about it, but if you have a positive attitude you can get through the bad times. I was lucky to have been brought up with such a philosophy and that really is the only reason I applied to go on the expedition. I knew that I could do it.

Sue:

So why me?

Perhaps this was the ultimate antidote to being a bored house-wife. Not that I actually had time to be one, though my husband would quite like one as a wife! Since getting married at twenty one to Jeremy, a solicitor, I had produced three children - Victoria, Philip and Edward - and have lived in the same house in Pattingham near Wolverhampton ever since. When the children had started at school, I needed to earn some money. I assessed my talents and decided to start up a catering business. This got busier and busier, so much so that the thought of having time to be bored was the ultimate pleasure.

I had also become very involved in carriage driving, and for six years was the national chairman of the carriage driving section of the Riding for the Disabled Association, which also seemed to take up more and more time, culminating in the running of the first International Driving Competition for the Disabled. We had competitors from six nations, including those as far afield as Argentina, Canada, the US, Sweden, Germany and Holland. It was very exciting and the whole competition had a wonderful atmosphere.

My other great venture was with my mother. We both went out to Jordan as guests of the Government, in order to teach the Bedouin at Petra the art of carriage driving. We had about a week's notice to prepare ourselves, yet another spur of the moment happening. We were going to do this because the Siq, the narrow gorge leading to the wonders of Petra, was becoming more and more polluted as those unable to walk or ride down were given lifts in vehicles, which in the narrow passage caused fumes and eroded the track. The answer was for the tourists to ride down in the carriages. The carriage builder, Michael Mart asked the two of us to go out, and we had a wonderful two weeks there, exploring Petra at will, and giving the driving lessons. One of the most magical places I have ever been to.

You could say there are really three main reasons why I found myself in the Arctic. The first one was that I felt that Victoria had issued a challenge, and who can resist a challenge - I felt very pleased that she obviously felt I was capable of doing this expedition, but mainly I felt very proud that she actually wanted me along with her. I knew that we had always got along with each other, and were indeed good friends, but to ask your mother!

Secondly, becoming fifty can give you a bit of a kick start into trying to do something different; the chance of a trip round the Equator might well have drawn the same response from me. It was not an age I was dreading, but a time of life that I felt needed to be marked by something. In fact I was quite looking forward to being fifty. No more do you have to worry about what people think of you. Even if you look fifty you only feel twenty five (though Jeremy does say if that is how old I feel, then I should

8

grow up a bit!).

For many women the age of fifty can be a time to dread. All the children have left home, your husband continues to come back from work every evening wanting dinner, and then afterwards you both complain how bad the television programmes are, so this should be instead a time for reassessment of your life, a time for change. Women are expected to be carers, which they are for the first half of their lives, but why shouldn't they go out and do something for themselves, in fact, be selfish? After I had made the decision to go I sometimes felt quite guilty about leaving Jeremy, who was naturally very worried, but I think that everyone needs 'own' time, when they do precisely what they want. In fact, I don't think it is selfish, it actually makes you a more relaxed person to live with, if you have achieved something in your own right.

The third cause of my saying yes was perhaps the main reason. Only six months before Victoria asked me, I had been diagnosed as having breast cancer and had a mastectomy. When lying in my hospital bed I had been thinking that this was the time for change. I made the decision to give up my catering business of nearly twenty years. This was a great relief, as I had been thinking of doing it for some time, but finding the excuse to do so was much harder. I also decided to do a course in Teaching English as a Second Language. I have always loved language, and I thought this might be less physically strenuous than cooking, and slightly more intellectual.

Cancer, for me, was when my whole world changed. Not because I ever for a moment thought I was going to die, but because your life suddenly takes on a different meaning and direction. You undergo the most undignified mammogram examination, then a few weeks later your doctor tells you there is a strong possibility that you have cancer. So what do you do? Your mind flies in every direction: what will happen, will it hurt, will you have to undergo endless treatment, perhaps losing your hair? Some years back having a mastectomy had been something that I had dreaded the thought of undergoing, but I have a marvellous friend, Ginny, who had undergone this operation, and one day when I was   staying there she had said 'do just look at my scar, it's so neat' and it was, and not really disfiguring, so from then on the dread left me, and I do feel incredibly grateful to her.

The surgeon told me that a biopsy had to be done, and that there was a week to wait for the results. I went straight off to my office Christmas party - a good cheering up exercise. Strangely enough, I did not feel desperately worried, because all along I had this knowledge that I would get better. I just wanted to know the results of the test. I felt that the person who was the most upset was Jeremy. Husbands are there on the sidelines; they worry for you, but feel very helpless and unable to do anything, but in fact he was an enormous help in just being incredibly supportive, as was Victoria. I should have liked to ring my mother and talk to her, but she rang me first to say that my father had broken his hip, so this was not the time for a talk!

Christmas was quite a tense time. We were in Scotland, Jeremy and Victoria knew but my parents and Philip and Edward did not. Eventually all were told. So a week after the biopsy, after we had got back from Christmas, the results came through. They were no surprise, and luckily I found I felt strong enough mentally to cope. But for a second the world does seem to stop for what seems like a lifetime. I had been preparing myself all the week before and knew deep down that a

10

mastectomy was going to be done. I am so glad, too, that I had a full mastectomy, as it was a bit like making a clean sweep, with nothing left behind; people I know who have had just bits out and always seem to have to go back for treatment. So when to have the operation? I had organised a New Year party and did not want to miss it, so I had a week to wait before it was done.

Victoria:

I think that Mum's positive attitude certainly helped us all at this stage. When you are told that your mother has cancer all you can think is that she is going to die. Seeing Mum though made me think "get your act together Victoria, stop feeling sorry for yourself, it's all going to be all right".

Sue:

The people who found it most difficult to comprehend were Philip and Edward. Men find this operation hard to relate to themselves, what is it like losing? In fact there is no comparison, one breast is not going to make a difference to anyone's life. Even if I had been younger I think that my attitude would have been the same, because I have been lucky enough to have a family who give me incredible support. One of the factors that helped me enormously was that my father lost his leg more than fifty years ago, and he has never complained and has always got on with doing what he wanted. I realised that one breast is nothing compared to this. Unlike him I would still be able to climb hills, go for long walks or play tennis. My mother also has a very positive attitude and was a great help; she is always 'definitely better' whatever is wrong!

11

The morning that I was due to go in I had a wonderful walk with the dogs and Philip, a last blast of fresh air before the air conditioned hospital. I felt slightly removed from everything on arrival, and really quite cheerful, though I think that the worse moment in any operation is the second before you are put under and you think: I hope they get the right one!

After the operation I still had the feeling that all was going to be well, and spent most of the time in hospital planning my next skiing trip, in eight weeks time. To have something to look forward to does help recovery. We laughed too, everyone was convinced that I would be lopsided and therefore ski round in circles the whole time, but by laughing at something bad you immediately remove the fear. More help came too from a friend, Sue Stirk and her reflexology, which is now becoming a treatment used post operatively in various hospitals. I felt so well and so healthy the entire time I was there, helped enormously by the cards I got, Sue Stirk's treatments and the wonderful support from friends. I had never before realised just what a boost 'Get Well' cards and flowers can give you.

I felt that this whole event was a turning point, and in retrospect I can honestly say that, for me, it was not a bad thing. I was so lucky to have the opportunity for change, much more good than ill has come out of having had cancer. Once you have had breast cancer you become incredibly aware of it and just how many people actually have this form of cancer. For me the great bonus of the expedition is having learned that I can speak in public and perhaps help those who are now waiting for treatment, or have just had it, and I hope I can show them that there is definitely life after cancer, and that there is nothing you cannot achieve.

Without cancer it is very unlikely that I would have gone on the expedition. So out of evil comes good. It makes life much more fun always to have a goal, you are never too old to want to achieve something else, however tiny an aim it is. So all I had to do was to get on with life with an immensely heightened awareness of the world around me, from flowers, skies, clouds, mountains to friends and family.

So there I was, this challenge in front of me. It took about two seconds to say yes. (Much better say yes and then work out how you are going to do it afterwards!). To have a chance of a real lifetime adventure handed to you like this was wonderful. I did have a few moments of doubt, but I always work by the principle: never say no to an opportunity because you might have regrets when you are eighty. I do not want to look back at my life and say 'if only'. Do as much as you can in the time allotted; you only have one go at life! I think too that I was perhaps trying to prove that nothing stops you, even if you have had cancer.

I was a little concerned about the fitness levels required, but as I have always led a pretty active life I was not too worried. Having been brought up on a farm, ridden horses, walked, climbed hills, bicycled and skied, I felt that a gentle walk to the North Pole would be fine! In fact I had no idea what I was in for, and, a bit like an ostrich I did not actually read any Arctic exploration books - perhaps I thought it might frighten me somewhat! Victoria did give me a photocopy of a part of Ranulph Fiennes' book and it sounded quite dreadful; unbearably cold and uncomfortable, not my scene at all! But the other reason that I read no books was to have no preconceived notions of what it would all be like, and in retrospect I am very glad I did not. Because now I am taking great pleasure in reading all the books, and thinking I've been there and done that, and some of it was worse, and some better, but it is me that is making the judgements.

For me perhaps the whole expedition was something that I seemed to do in rather a casual frame of mind, it all just happened. I think that being an optimist is a plus when something like the proposed expedition is mooted. Jeremy was very worried, but I knew that I would be all right - perhaps foolhardy, but that is the difference between optimism and pessimism. Jeremy is always pleasantly surprised if things work out, but not disappointed if they do not. I know that if they do not work out this time, they will next time, and I have not been disappointed yet.

After this there was a slight anticlimax, nothing seemed to happen. I went to France on holiday, and nearly forgot about it. But Victoria had been busy organising application forms, which she eventually sent me in September. I remember showing it to Jeremy, who was horrified. He had not really taken in the fact that I really meant what I had said about the expedition. The information that came with the application form was obviously composed for publicity, and not to comfort husbands. It discussed ravening hordes of polar bears, breaking ice, discomfort and hardship. We had to write about ourselves and why we wanted to be considered for the expedition. I just scribbled down a few things about myself, it was hard to know what to put. After all, I had not exactly done much in the way of polar exploration. In fact, I had barely camped, had never carried a rucksack, and had not really done anything particularly outward bound before.

Victoria:

I think at this stage that Dad thought it was all my fault and that I had persuaded Mum to come with me, but anyone who knows Mum would realise that she makes up her own mind for herself!

Sue:

Again, another period of not much happening. We went to various parties, and I thought that perhaps it was time to bring out into the open what I wanted to do. We were having dinner with friends, and in passing I said that I hoped to be selected for an expedition to the North Pole. I do not think Jeremy had really listened during the past few months when we had talked about it, or perhaps he had just pushed it to the back of his mind because he didn't want it to happen, but at the party he actually said: 'in no way are you going to do this'. Perhaps I should have listened, as a good wife, but by then I was becoming enthused. Maybe Jeremy thought that this was a mid life crisis and would go away. So I said I would go along to the selection weekend, as it was bound to be a lot of super fit women, Gladiator types, and I would be much too old, which he seemed to think would be fine!

Victoria:

For me, life was following a similar pattern. Having told my friends and company what I was planning to do I just carried on as usual. I did find though that I was often introduced as 'that crazy person I told you about who wants to walk to the North Pole'. It was usually quite a conversation stopper.

Sue:

Christmas 1995 came and went. Too much food and drink; not the sort of diet for would be Arctic explorers about to set out on a selection weekend. I had to go and buy a pair of walking boots, never having had a pair before - in the past I had just worn trainers! I had to borrow a rucksack and find the right equipment to go walking on Dartmoor on a bitter January weekend, to compete with about eighty other hopeful women.

Chapter Two

Survival of the Fittest

Sue:

It was rather like arriving at a new school. We turned up at Newton Abbot station, on a bitterly cold evening. One hardly dared complain - after all we all wanted to go to the Arctic, so a touch of frost should be nothing! There was a whole convoy of cars, taking us off to Wydemeet (the home of Pen and Mary Hadow and HQ of the Polar Travel Company), to meet up with the other hopefuls. Everyone was tired, and slightly Friday nightish after several hours on hot trains, to arrive - in driving rain, pitch black dark - amongst a seething hoard of other women, all of whom were in competition with you. Although it must be said that at this stage, knowing nothing about the expedition, we were not yet taking it particularly seriously!

We were welcomed by Mary Hadow, Pen's wife, who was in charge of making sure that the right people had turned up. We were ushered into a huge barn with bales of straw piled up, and arranged into a form of lecture theatre seating. The best thing was that we were all given a glass or two of mulled wine. It was wonderful; suddenly everything seemed rosy, and all these women now seemed not at all threatening.

Victoria and I were whisked away to be interviewed for a television documentary, little realising that this was to be the start of many such happenings. The media all latched on to the mother / daughter bit - very scary the first time around, but it was incredible how soon you got used to dealing with them.

Victoria:

Back in the barn, it was comforting, there was not a Gladiator in sight! Not the super fit twenty year old's we were expecting, but ordinary women, some of them even quite plump. They were certainly not fitness freaks - one even carried her handbag with her during the selection activities. She was not selected! Others put on make up, which did not look too good later on when it had run in the rain.

Sue:

It was an interesting evening in the barn. Everyone had this common dream, a sort of idea of something that we all wanted to do, but it was still at the stage of being not quite real. The whole weekend had this slightly surreal feeling. We all started introducing ourselves, and what really came out of all this was - why *can't* women do something like this? We have been told for many years that this is not a female environment, but why? Who has been out and done it? Only the men, and they do not know whether we can or cannot do it. Gradually a sort of excitement began to build up. Here was something really exciting, worthwhile, we could put our mark in the books of exploration. Our briefing gave us a few basic facts of polar exploration, and what we would be expected to do over the weekend, but it was all quite relaxed.

We woke up to cameras being thrust in our faces, not the sort of waking up call to be recommended. Victoria never looks her best in the morning, and somehow managed to be there in front of the camera and answer questions coherently! We had passed a night of fitful sleep. The evening before we had rearranged the bales of straw so the entire floor was covered, and then put our sleeping bags on top, two bales per person.

18

Quite a squash, given the numbers there, but the heat from the bodies probably kept us a little warmer.

I had had to borrow Philip's sleeping bag, I felt that this had been to many parties, judging by the smell of beer and wine, plus other unidentifiable smells that I did not want to know about. The smells practically knocked you out if you put your head down into it. This was my first night ever in a sleeping bag. It could have been a lot worse. I did wake up at one stage in the night, positive there was something creeping in my hair. I knew that the dogs caught ticks from the straw that they slept on when in the stables, so I was a trifle concerned that I would wake up to find my head covered in these horrible things. I was not sure whether it was better or worse in the morning finding that it was caterpillars, thousands of little green caterpillars, all woken up by the hot air that we were breathing. I thought that I was marginally fonder of caterpillars than ticks, but only just!

Victoria:

Having spent numerous nights camping on the moors of Otterburn or at Catterick Garrison whilst in the university Officer Training Corps, all this was far less of a shock to me. Sleeping in a barn was a pleasant surprise and I have to admit to wondering if the selection weekend was going to be tough enough to sort out the good from the bad. In retrospect this was a very arrogant attitude, because those who had not been in the army were no less capable than people who had had the opportunity. The sense of camaraderie though was wonderful and something that I had really missed since giving up the OTC.

Sue:

We all had breakfast, but not very big, as we were all feeling a little nervous. We had been divided into five teams of fifteen each to make the activities more manageable. Victoria and I were in the same one but had decided that, even though we would like to, it would be better not to talk to each other too much. (However, we did drift together occasionally.) We were led by an incredible man - Rob Dixon, who could lead you over Dartmoor blindfolded. Later on he was the only guide who knew Dartmoor well enough to be able to lead us to safety once the weather had deteriorated. As we left Wydemeet the mist was right down. It was one of those winter days when it never gets truly light, and night comes very early. We walked, with no clear idea of where we were going and because the weather had become so bad you could not see anything (in retrospect, rather like the Arctic).

After two or three hours walking we were getting to know our team mates. In our team we had Rosie Stancer, who was subsequently selected, and Sue Self, who trained with us at Resolute and was the reserve. We also had a couple of journalists, one from the *Express* and one from *The Times*, who did not know what she was being sent on, had not got the right kit, and ended up with the most appalling blisters. Eventually we all met up round about midday, and there was the Press again. They played a very important part in bringing the expedition to the public eye, and Pen hoped this would help with sponsorship .

We climbed a small hill and had to run down, looking - well, I was not quite sure how we were meant to look, just fit and healthy we thought. Pen then appeared, and showed us a rather fast flowing, cold looking river and said: 'over we go'. So we followed our leader, getting

20

extremely wet; Victoria up to her bra line, me up to my thighs. It was cold, but the press got their photographs, which is what it was all about, nothing to do with our fitness. When we had got out, and rung out our clothes, squeezed our socks dry, put our boots back on with fumbly fingers trying to do up the laces, we were given wonderful venison pasties, solid, but filling and energy giving. We picked at the rest of our food, and had a drink, and were ready for the off again.

Victoria:

The photo that appeared in most of the Sunday papers the next day was 'Mother pulling daughter from raging torrent'. It required a lot of imagination to make the river a raging torrent, but we soon learnt that the press use a great deal of artistic licence.

Sue:

At this stage, midday, the drizzle had let up a little, so when we got moving again our clothes began to dry, but this did not last long. The drizzle turned to rain, and it was a very soggy group of women walking; morale was low. In the gloomy half light we came to the river again, and this time it was the turn of those who had somehow managed to avoid getting wet the first time to get in the water and cross the river, and then back again.

We now decided, as the dark was rapidly coming down, that all the groups should actually join up. In retrospect this was not a good thing. It was like moving a juggernaut. Eighty of us all walking at the pace of the slowest, some had torches, some did not. The slow ones were now getting very tired, we were right at the front and found that we

21

sometimes had to wait nearly ten minutes for the back markers to catch up. The rain was still coming down and it had even started to sleet. But we were potential Arctic explorers, so this should be no problem! You could not complain and seem like a wimp; we were the tough ones. At least, we thought we were. We still had no idea of what we were letting ourselves in for.

Eventually, about twelve hours after leaving Wydemeet we came to Nuns Cross Farm, a ruined house which is used by campers on Dartmoor. But it was locked, so we all sheltered round the sides, away from the wind and the driving rain. At this stage we were meant to walk back to Wydemeet across a mire, which sounded very 'Hound of the Baskervilles'. But with this number of people moving so slowly, it was deemed not to be safe. We both knew that we would have been able to do it if we could have walked at a decent pace, but going so slowly you did get cold. You longed to have a bracingly fast walk to warm up. Sheltering at the farm you could see this army of women, some of whom (the less fit ones) were becoming hypothermic. It was the sort of cold when your bones are chilled the whole way through and your knee caps shake uncontrollably.

When I thought I would have a quick hot drink out of my thermos I found that my tea bags had disintegrated in the wet and the water had got cold. Not the best time for this to happen. Others tried to light up damp cigarettes for comfort, and even if they were dry, the wind was blowing too much for the lighters to work! What was decided was that everyone would be transported back to Wydemeet but, as this was obviously going to take time, a number of us decided to start walking; anything was better than just waiting. So we set off for Princetown. From my point of view this was the best thing we could have done. We got warm, and therefore marginally less wet, but Victoria was having problems with her feet and had started to develop blisters.

However, after about three quarters of an hour we arrived in Princetown, and there was a pub - and even better, someone in our group had some money. I have never downed a whisky-mac quicker! The worst bit was trying to go to the loo. All our fingers had got so cold and wet that they did not seem to function properly, and undoing a zip was near to impossible. We had a few dryish things in our rucksacks, and so put something else on, but most of our clothes were still extremely wet. The pub residents seemed slightly bemused by this influx of rather wet women!

Victoria:

This was the worst part of the weekend. I had appalling blisters and was cold and wet. All sense of camaraderie had gone. No one was talking to anyone and for me talking, singing and laughing keeps spirits up no matter how dreadful the conditions - something we were to experience regularly once up in the Arctic. The walk to Princetown was one of the hardest in my life and it required all my self discipline not to stop. Mum was miles ahead by this stage and I think that was the final straw. How dare she be fitter than me? I am twenty three years younger for goodness sake. Of course it was not fitness but mental attitude, and that is where we make a great team, I may have youth on my side but Mum is probably far stronger mentally.

Sue:

I had been quite worried as to how I would cope with carrying the rucksack because of the mastectomy scar. In the end I actually cut up an old sheepskin coat which I whisked away from the dogs, who had been sleeping on it at home, and I made it into sort of pads, which I put under the straps. In fact I need not have worried, there seemed to be no ill effects. My arm, which still had not quite got 100% movement back, was fine, and so was the scar. Victoria was very good, and kept an eye on how I was doing.

Victoria:

I found that throughout all the selection weekends and whilst on the expedition itself I became very protective of Mum and hated to see her lag behind or go too far ahead. I wanted to be near her in case anything happened.

Sue:

We eventually had our lift back to Wydemeet, and Pen had organised that there would be giant blowers, in front of which we could dry. Just standing there was a luxury; never mind the hot bath, this was wonderful. We were given a warming plate of stew, and then more information. The problem for me was that I am definitely a morning person, and having been walking all those hours was ready for bed, so I had very little memory of what was said! I did not even notice the smell of the sleeping bag this time.

The next morning came early, with (yet again) the video cameras watching our every waking moment. We looked dreadful. Tousled hair, dirty hands, probably rather smelly, not the sort of sight that husbands or boyfriends would have wanted to see! Breakfast as the day

24

before, and then we were divided into groups again. This time we were told the finer points of navigation, and were given some map references to find. Rosie Stancer was the one who started, and we had to find an old cross on the hill. It was in a way magic when we arrived at the stone. Rosie was as excited as if she had found the crock of gold at the end of the rainbow and indeed it felt like that to all of us who had never used a compass before, or known how to take bearings. We drifted from point to point, and then arrived back at the house, packed up and set off to the pub.

Pubs seem to play a very important part in the whole expedition: decisions were made there, information given out or just recovery drinks! Pen asked us in a slightly desultory way if we still wanted to go the Arctic. Some of the prospective walkers did say no, but most of us were even more eager than before; our appetites had been whetted. Eventually we all made our way to the station, or drove off home, and as we said goodbye to each other we felt that we had actually made really good friends. We were slightly in limbo as to what came next. Was the expedition still on, how would they reduce us to the required number, and indeed, when was the next selection going to be, as we did need to train slightly more vigorously for it. So home we went, tired but on a high with the excitement of the whole concept.

Victoria:

I was greeted at Paddington station by my boyfriend and taken to my flat in London longing for a hot bath, only to discover that my flatmate David, had used all the hot water. To this day I have never forgiven him! Next morning I was whisked off at some ungodly hour to

Radio Five to be interviewed live on their breakfast show. It was so early in the morning that I was too sleepy to be nervous, and the worst thing of all was that no one even heard me because it was broadcast at 6.45 am!

Sue:

Again we had another period of not much happening, Caroline and Pen were trying to drum up sponsors, which was proving a problem. Originally Pen had said that it would be quite easy, but as time went by we discovered that not many companies were keen to have anything to do with an expedition of women going to a man's environment, where no woman had trod before. Companies do not mind sponsoring rugger teams, golf matches, yacht races or art exhibitions - but a bunch of women going off to the Arctic - well, no thank you, no help. A sponsor had to be found though, to fund the second and final selection weekend. Neutrogena came up trumps: they provided the cash, and a wonderful supply of all their face cream, hand cream and body lotion. They have now gained twenty life long supporters!

So we had the date of the weekend, which we were told was to be a weekend from hell! Training suddenly became quite important. My problem was that we would only get back from holiday five days before the weekend, and how was I going to be at my peak fitness after two and a half weeks of French wine and food? Cycling was the answer, so every evening all the spotted Normandy cows with their crumpled horns watched me whizzing by. Sometimes Jeremy came with me, it is a wonderful way to see the countryside. There have been a lot of secondary benefits from the expedition and the fitness regime.

Victoria:

I had the best training for the final selection weekend. Again in France, but I was in the Alps spending a week summer skiing, climbing and white water rafting. Every morning I could be seen staggering (not running) up all the windy roads back to the chalet where I was staying!

*

Sue:

It was September 1996 and the weekend from hell (in actuality four days) had arrived, and far quicker than most of us wanted, though we did want to be put out of our misery. We had arranged to meet in Bristol, Victoria was going to pick me up from the train. But were we going to get there? She arrived at the station in clouds of exhaust fumes and with a noise fit to waken the dead. Her exhaust was broken. We decided that we should be all right, but within three miles felt that we definitely would NOT be all right. So we limped over the Avon bridge to the nearest service station, where miraculously there was a garage which would actually mend the exhaust, but it would take an hour or so.

Luckily we had allowed time to have one last gorge of food, as we had been told there would be nothing to eat that evening. So into the Little Chef, and a pig out of energy giving food. The mechanic did his stuff, and we were on our way.

Victoria:

This is where it helps to be a woman, I very emotionally described what was wrong with my car and where we where going. I doubt the mechanic believed my tearful explanation of needing to get to Dartmoor to go to the North Pole, but I am eternally grateful to him for giving us the benefit of the doubt.

Sue:

We were more than a little worried about how we would cope. There had been an article in that day's *Times*, with a picture of Rosie and her trainer, also a terrifying quote from Pen: - 'We want to break down all their defences and see who is still full of enthusiasm and team spirit. It will be heartbreaking for those who don't make it but we couldn't choose between them without doing something like this.' His aim was to 'scare them rigid'. We were nervous, worried and not a little apprehensive as to whether we had the right kit, enough food, too much food, the right first aid, even our boots, would they be all right this time round? At the same time we were very excited, with butterflies in the stomach and on a sort of high, as this could be the start of something incredibly challenging.

It was lovely both of us being in the car together, as we could talk our worries through, and there was not the competition between us that there probably was between the others. It was after all a question of the survival of the fittest, in every sense. The whole weekend stretching in front of us seemed to be appearing in a sort of glow, because the weather was wonderful - one of those glorious September days that gives a golden haze to the world. Dartmoor looked warm and welcoming, so different from the weekend in January. We knew that we both felt we could do it, and would be picked if things went our way. We knew that mentally we were strong but it was the unknown, not knowing what would be thrown at us in the way of challenges, that kept us just a little bit tense.

We arrived at Kelly College in Tavistock around five o'clock that evening and it was wonderful to meet all our friends from January again. A newcomer was Lucy Roberts, who had missed the initial week-end. Sue Fullilove flew in that afternoon from Africa, where she was doing orthopaedics. Rosie turned up looking incredibly fit, armed with a supply of delicious goodies which we all shared. We soon got used to always having yummy food from Harvey Nichols when Rosie was around! We had to put our kit out and have it checked. In retrospect, we all had far too much food. We both left some behind, but my rucksack still seemed to weigh a ton compared to Rosie's and one or two others. On the other hand, I am quite big and strong, and needed the extra comfort!

We were given our briefing in the college, and the first thing that was done was to collect all our watches. We never realised just how much we would miss not having a watch until that weekend. Automatically your glance keeps dropping down to your wrist. We all became slightly obsessive about the time, to the extent that when journalists or photographers appeared we tried to look at their wrists, but they had been told they were not to let us know the time. We were briefed on navigation, map reading and taking compass bearings, a lot to take in during a short period.

About nine o'clock, though of course we really had no idea of the time, we were all bundled into various vehicles and dumped, in our groups, on the moor. Victoria was in a different one to me, for which we were actually quite glad. We could do our own thing without worrying about the other one, and you could be who you wanted, instead of Victoria's mother or Sue's daughter. We set off in what seemed incredible darkness, carrying a six foot wooden pole, which had to come with us at all times and was a sort of test of team spirit and how we would cope with a useless object. We called ours Paula the Pole, and actually, in the end became quite attached to her! We felt that she had to be feminine, this being an all women expedition!

Within half an hour or so we came to our first climb, an enormous pile of rocks disappearing up into the darkness. There was a rope to help, but it was a very steep pull up, particularly as we all had our fully laden rucksacks. I felt that I was being pulled backwards by the sheer weight of the rucksack, and also had the worry, at the bottom of the rocks, as to whether my arm would have the muscle power to pull me up, as when I had my mastectomy the muscles had been moved around, and I had the lymph glands out as well, which could have affected my strength. But both arms felt equally strong, and I found I could get to the top easily, and in fact was able to help some of the others as I was first up. Funnily enough there was no fear, though one of our team members did find this exercise particularly difficult as her fiancé had been killed in front of her doing a similar climb. But she showed great fortitude and managed to get to the top. This was the first of many such tests which were thrown at us over the course of the weekend.

Victoria:

Our team also had a pole but decided that it was to be a man and we therefore called it various unprintable names. The only way to describe these poles is to imagine a telegraph pole and shorten it slightly. Totally impossible to drag around the place.

I hated being separated from Mum, not knowing where she was and wondering if she was OK. Apparently Mum was not too concerned

30

about me!

Sue:

The next ordeal was the abseil. Something I had always wanted to do, but had never had the opportunity. It was one of the most exciting parts of the whole weekend. Imagine throwing yourself off a cliff when you cannot see the bottom. It was totally dark with a few stars twinkling, you step up to the edge of the cliff not knowing what is below you, attach the safety harness and launch yourself over the edge. The initial step is terrifying, but you have got to trust the person holding the rope at the top. But the thrill was wonderful. Eventually all the teams got to the bottom, but no-one knew what to do next. Part of the testing, we thought. Did we have time to eat something, or even light our stoves and cook, or should we just wait for orders?

In the end we were all moved on, out of a quarry, which was like a lunar landscape with boulders tumbled all over the floor, to a flatter area where we had an auction of useful items for what remained of the night! Each team bid for things like ropes, tarpaulins and more poles.

Our team ended up with two extra poles, one tarpaulin and a length of rope with which we rigged up a sort of awning against the cliff edge. It was incredibly stony, and quite hard to sleep, and all our breaths condensed and dripped on us, as well as the water running down the cliff edge. Victoria's team doubled up their tarpaulin and slept on top of half and under the other half, they felt it was much quicker as no construction was required, and sure enough were the first team to be ready for bed. It was a wonderful night, frosty, clear moonlight and you could see shooting stars appearing at intervals.

We had been told that we were going to have to move off at five o'clock, but WHEN was five o'clock? No watches, so how could we guess? We still do not know what time we actually got up, but someone started moving, and the rest of us stumbled out of our sleeping bags and started trying to find flattish pieces of ground to put our stoves on in order to brew up some breakfast.

It was a glorious morning, a touch of frost, the sun beginning to come up, a slight mist in the valleys, and scattered over the moor were some black cattle. As we set off we all felt full of the most boundless energy. We had redivided into our groups again. I did not even see Victoria, though I had heard her voice in the distance, but by now we had all become real teams, and we stuck to our group, and to our constant companion Paula the Pole. We walked for some time, impossible to tell how long, the timelessness of the days seems to be another thread running through all the weekends and the actual expedition. Whether you felt tired physically was much more important than whether it was actually supper time, bed time or getting up time.

It must have been quite early on our second day, say about ten o'clock, when we arrived at a lake in the middle of the moor, seemingly surrounded by the nation's photographers who appeared to line the entire lake. This was to be a photo-opportunity, fifty or so women, perhaps even stripping off to swim across the lake! How disappointed they must have been to discover we were doing this fully clothed, boots and all, pulling our rucksacks behind us, protected by bin liners! The water was very warm, and extremely murky, probably dozens of dead sheep resting on the sludgy mud we had to wade through to get into the deep water. But not a problem.

I had a slight mishap with the sheepskin with which I had protected my scar; it floated away, as did my false boob, in a polythene bag (I had put it in the bag before getting into the water as I thought it would take some time to dry if it got wet, and would therefore be rather uncomfortable!) I managed to rescue the boob, but not the sheepskin, and from then on did not bother, and had no problems. I did not use my smart silicone boob, as I thought that if it got punctured it might be a bit messy and expensive to replace! Victoria removed her boots for the swim, and managed to cut her foot on some unidentifiable object at the bottom of the lake. Quite a nasty gash, but it did not stop her!

Victoria:

One eager cameraman even stripped off to his bare essentials in order to film us from the water. Unfortunately it just led to us taking pictures of him filming us!

Sue:

We dried off in the September sunshine, by now a lovely warm autumn morning. Luckily we had some dry spares and so put them on, though the boots were thoroughly wet. But once we started walking they did not take long to dry off. So yet again we got going in our teams.

We walked down a road and arrived at a little hump back bridge where waiting in front of us, cameras at the ready, were the nation's press again. This time we had to run, with rucksacks bouncing, and of course the ubiquitous pole for every group. The press were not satisfied with the first run, and we had to do it again. Everyone felt that they were happy to do anything they were asked if it would help raise the profile of the expedition, and help with our selection.

Having done this little scamper we had to climb up the quite steep slope of Sheepstor Tor. In any circumstances it is a wonderful hill to climb as you have stunning views from the top. Half way up we were both stopped by a photographer, who must have taken excellent photographs because of the backdrop (sadly we never saw them). This was rather a relief, as it was a chance to catch our breath. The whole weekend was spent trying to hide any breathlessness and appear incredibly fit.

At the top of the hill each team was given a mobile telephone. This was a publicity stunt to try and find more sponsors, we tried various large companies. There was some interest, but no one was too sure of what actually came out of it. We had yet more photographs, by now we were beginning to learn who would be chosen to be in front of the camera. It was always Caroline Hamilton, the expedition organiser, Rosie Stancer, the Queen Mother's great niece, Ann Daniels, who was the mother of triplets, and Sue and Victoria Riches, mother and daughter! We hoped the others did not feel too annoyed with these endless photo calls, we were all very conscious that we were always being picked out, but if the publicity helped in the fund-raising we were very happy to do it.

The time at the top of the Tor was rather like a big picnic party - everyone was eating, drinking, some even brewing up, and the sunshine helped to create some sort of party atmosphere. I enjoyed catching up with Victoria and finding out how she had done.

After this rest period, which seemed to last an incredibly long time, we started off again. But within five minutes we were sitting down, doing self analysis. Looking at pictures of various cartoon characters and saying which one best represented what we felt like, and who all the

34

others were like! By now we were all quite honest with each other, and it gave me quite a boost to discover that the others saw me as a smiling friendly person! Then on to being blindfolded and having to make a perfect square, with only the help of a piece of rope. As with the whole of the weekend, we spent a lot of time laughing at ourselves, and we wished we could have seen what we were doing.

Victoria:

To make the perfect square you fold the piece of rope into half and then half again. Three people take one corner each and the fourth person takes the two ends. You then sit on the ground with your legs at right angles and hold the rope so it aligns with all the right angles and there you have your perfect square - in theory!

Sue:

The whole of the day passed in a kind of idyllic blur. The wonderful sunshine, the heat, getting to know the other would be explorers, the feeling of comradeship. At times we were very conscious that we were being watched and assessed all the time, and you almost bent over backwards to be seen to be helping someone! Even at this stage each team did have members who were obviously less able, and who did need some help and encouragement.

Our observer/guide, Jack Russell was a charming man, and a pleasure to walk with. We knew that he had to be nice with a name like that, and three of them at home! At times I did feel a bit of a granny, I realised that I was more prepared to say what I thought, without being so worried about the consequences. I knew that I wanted to go, but I felt that if not picked so be it, it just wasn't meant. As a result I felt very laid back about the whole weekend, and was just hugely enjoying myself. Some of the others were deadly serious about being chosen, and there was a lot of raw emotion around when the final teams were actually read out. This sounds as if I did not really want to go, but I did. Very badly. But I was quite prepared to go along with the decision of the organisers. After all, they were the experts.

So we gently wended our way towards a familiar place - Nuns Cross Farmhouse - but how different this time. It seemed warm and welcoming - quite a contrast to the previous visit! On the way there we had stunning views of the sea towards Plymouth. Jack, and perhaps he should not have done this, warned me that at some stage during the night there would be some form of exercise, or excitement. It did not actually make any difference my knowing, but at least I was semi-prepared. He was not too happy with the actual format of the weekend. At Kelly College they run a number of outward bound weekends and corporate weeks with Jack in charge, so in actual fact he did know what he was talking about. There seemed to be quite a conflict of interest between Pen and Jack, but in all honesty it was Pen's weekend, and he had been to the Arctic, which Jack had not.

Just before we arrived at the farmhouse we came across a lone tent, with someone brewing up his supper. He must have been horrified to discover that during his weekend of peace and quiet in the loneliness of Dartmoor there were about fifty women just up the hill from him. All of us cooking our own little suppers. Some people did seem to have the most revolting mixtures, some mixed their meat and pudding together, others ate strange looking healthy options! One food fact we did learn:

take a malt loaf with you to nibble on during the day. It has very high energy. As the sun went down we all found places to put our sleeping bags in the house. We settled down with our own teams, in different rooms.

Victoria:

I was thoroughly enjoying myself at this stage. I had a great team and we were working really well together. I was also being very philosophical - like Mum I knew that I was more than capable, but ultimately the Polar Travel Company knew best and I would trust their judgement.

Sue:

We did not know how long we had been asleep when suddenly the house filled with smoke, a lot of shouting and yelling: "Get out, get out!" We gathered up our bits and got dressed, luckily mentally prepared for whatever might happen. We got outside, and were told that there were four or five injured people out on the moor, and that we had to rescue them within fifteen minutes! We split up into parties with torches for signalling, and went out to find the injured, which we did without too much of a problem. We did think of the poor solitary camper whose night time peace was rent asunder with groups of women trampling, shouting and wandering about!

The injured were taken back to the farmhouse, and we were told that the next test was to be a race. We could leave our rucksacks, but were still wearing our boots; not quite running gear. Everyone walked up to the road, and then we were off. We both ran together, which helped with our speed. I was very touched that Victoria reduced her pace for me. We had to run a set distance out, check in at the far point, and then run back. By the end we were overtaking quite a number of people, Victoria sprinted the last bit, and was about ninth. I managed to come in eleventh, not too bad.

So back to bed for what was left of the night, but still with no idea of the time. We struggled to a state of wakefulness, fairly early in the morning one would imagine, and went outside to cook our breakfast. Yet another glorious autumn morning, our third day. A touch of frost, incredible clarity of light and not a cloud in the sky. I felt marvellous, not an ache or pain, my feet felt they could go on for ever, unlike Victoria. Her foot was in quite a bad way, partly due to the deep gash from swimming in the lake (which had had stitches put in it), and partly from blisters. But she is very strong minded and she knew that nothing would prevent her walking as much as was required.

We then had to gather round Pen, who was going to reallocate the teams. It began to be obvious as to who was on the shortlist and in the running for selection. Victoria was now put with me, plus some others who we really did not know - Lucy Roberts for one, also Ann Daniels, whom we really enjoyed getting to know; great fun and a good sense of humour. Each of our teams was given a ready to assemble bookcase! Also a plan, and ten minutes to work out how to assemble it, then we would be timed putting it together. We actually found this one of the most interesting exercises, because what were obviously the three best teams made their bookcases far quicker than what you might call the 'b' teams. And we had to do it twice, but with the same results. The team work was already beginning to show itself.

Yet again we set off, but after twenty minutes another halt, more

38

interviews, ridiculous questions - such as, if the worst came to the worst, would we eat each other? Well, who knows what situations would arise, we would prefer not to, and we didn't think that things would get that bad, (but I had just watched the film 'Alive' three weeks before, so was quite conscious that in appalling conditions anything goes). Lots of posed pictures, and then (rather a relief) on with the walking. We realised that all this stop/starting was in fact part of the testing process. The sun was well up by now, and it was getting fairly hot. Luckily all the streams were running, so we could top up our water bottles as often as we wanted.

We again had Jack Russell as our leader, and at one stage we were joined by Oliver Shepherd, one of Ranulph Fiennes' trans-globe companions. We were made to do odder and odder things, like carrying Jack on the pole (which was still with us), crawling through ditches, and carrying stones for some way. We were still all very aware that we must show the team spirit, but it was much easier this time as - apart from one person who actually left us by mid morning - we were all of an equal standard of fitness.

We had been given all the map references for where we were meant to go, and each person or pair of people took it in turns to navigate. Ann and I did it together; we were all right, though not brilliant. We did not go the most direct route as at this stage as we still had our slow team member, and she was finding the tussocky grass a big problem. She kept saying 'don't wait for me' but if you are together you cannot just leave someone on the middle of Dartmoor. Eventually she left us at a halt.

Luckily, the weather was so clear we could see exactly where we were aiming for, which made life a lot easier. We had to ford a river, the Dart, but were only allowed to get one team member wet. Lucy volunteered. She had the most terrible blisters, and to cool them seemed a wonderful idea, so we used our rope, the pole, and Lucy. It was quite a problem getting across without being pulled into the river by the weight of our rucksacks, which we had loosened so that if we did fall in we would not be held underwater by them. We had yet more pep talks asking if we knew what we were letting ourselves in for? We all said yes. Admittedly, we did not really have an idea of what the Arctic Ocean could possibly be like, but at that stage we were all so hyped up with the idea of the Relay that we would have done, or said, anything!

By now the third day was beginning to turn to dusk, yet we still seemed to be plodding on, rather weary by now. Both Victoria and Lucy had bad blisters, but were pretending that they did not exist. We were made to carry one of the journalists up a steep hill in a sort of make shift stretcher, it was hard work as she was very solid! We got to the top, and there was a wonderful sunset which made up for the awfulness of the last half hour.

It was now getting quite dark, and this was the moment that I was so glad Victoria was there. We walked together, and discussed what had happened, the people with us and what was the likelihood of our being selected. We went through those we thought would be, and our feelings about them. We both felt we were in with a very good chance. We knew that physically we could do it, and that we were strong mentally. It was just a question as to whether the organisers liked us.

We came down to the river, black in the dark. We had to pick our way across some stones, and walked along the riverside with the cold dropping down, almost freezing, as it does on clear September nights after a hot day. Eventually we arrived back at Wydemeet, to find that all

40

the others had been back for quite some time. They had all decided to sleep under tarpaulins on the hillside and some went off to the pub. Our little lot felt that we would much rather go to bed.

We settled down in a small hut, eased our aching limbs, administered to the agonising blisters and had a quick clean up, such as we could with cold water. We chatted in a desultory fashion, no one quite liked to say whether they thought they had a chance, skirting round the subject, talking about anything except the North Pole. A slightly wild Scottish woman, Morag Howell, the radio communications expert (who with her husband is involved in most Arctic and Antarctic expeditions) suddenly came in and asked if we could shoot - polar bears being the worry apparently. We both said yes, so did some of the others. She said they were having major difficulties choosing the team - the kitchen at Wydemeet was the nerve centre of the selection process.

Victoria:

To me it was also becoming more apparent that we could well be chosen. We had had to walk a much further distance than the other teams that day, and in some ways the pressure seemed to be greater. It was lovely to be offered the hut rather than camp outside, as compensation for having walked further than the others. By this stage I had decided that I had done my best, and all would be determined within the next few hours. So I spent the evening drinking the contents of my hipflask which I had not dared drink previously for fear of not being at my best.

Sue:

Eventually we all went to sleep, still rather smelly, and woke up

41

with real butterflies in our stomachs - an aching, frightened, optimistic/ pessimistic feeling. I had a cup of tea, the others could manage nothing. I realised that being older you can cope more easily with the waiting and the worrying.

So into the barn - where it all had started in January and would finish for some - to hear whose names would be read out. Great emotion and tension were hanging in the air. Little groups stood together, hardly any talking. Pen came in. Silence. He said that they had sat up half the night to list the chosen few, as it was such a difficult task.

No press were present as Pen felt that there could be drama. He started alphabetically, so by the time that he had got to the 'm' we both felt that he had a full team. Then my name - Victoria said this was the worse moment - suppose that they did not say hers; suppose I was picked, and she was not. I had said all along that if they did not pick me I would quite understand. But the other way round? It seemed a pause of about two minutes, but can only have been seconds, but, Victoria's name was next.

Victoria:

It is impossible to describe that fifteen minute period of my life. Even now my stomach gets butterflies thinking about it. As they read out the names I heard Mum's and not mine, and I was convinced that they had got to the maximum required. In my excitement I had forgotten that Sue comes before Victoria in the alphabet. I have never felt so excited, terrified, and (because of those not chosen) guilty. I just wanted to tell the world. We were both going to the North Pole.

Chapter Three

Media, Money & Muscles

The Relay Team -

Rose Agnew (50): a teacher with three grown up children

Karen Bradburn (37): an air stewardess with BA

Andre Chadwick (33): a teacher of English to foreign business men

Lynne Clarke (36): mother of two and a quantity surveyor

Catherine Clubb (28): a freelance outward bound instructor

Ann Daniels (31): mother of triplets, ex-bank worker

Sue Fullilove (31): an orthopaedic surgeon in London

Claire Fletcher (31): a chiropractor

Caroline Hamilton (33): a film financier, whose brainchild the whole expedition was

Zoe Hudson (30): a sports physiotherapist, could be useful!

Sarah Jones (28): a PE teacher and marathon runner

Jan McCormac (27): a Royal Protection police officer

Juliette May (33): a business development officer with a baby son

Pom Oliver (44): a film producer

Paula Power (30): works in IT

Lucy Roberts (28): a journalist and lighting designer, also a marathon runner

Emma Scott (21): a student

Rosie Stancer (35): PR manager (whose grandfather had missed Scott's Antarctic expedition because he was too large to fit in the tent, but her husband William's grandfather had been with Shackleton)

Finally, **Victoria** (27): and **Sue** (51): the oldest on the expedition.

Sue:

Now was the elation, the tears, the commiseration. Suddenly it was going to happen; this dream was going to materialise, this nebulous idea to become solid fact. I do not think any of us knew quite how this was going to affect the rest of our lives and the lives of our families. Suddenly we became two groups of people, the chosen and the rejected. We stood there, what should we do next? That was decided quite quickly, we would go back to Kelly College and have a shower. We were incredibly dirty, smelly and generally rather disgusting! Not at all nice women to know, and as we were about to meet the press it was better that we should look slightly more normal and smell fresher than fresh. Later on when we said to Pen that the whole weekend was much easier than we had anticipated, his reply was that if you found it easy, you were the sort of person they wanted; if it was hard, you would not be able to cope.

Victoria:

So often the families of those who go off on adventures are forgotten. It is without a doubt hardest for them as they have to sit at home waiting and hoping, no doubt thinking the worst. Mum and I are both aware that we neglected Dad at times, probably when he most needed us, and was feeling anxious about the forthcoming trip. It is very difficult not to get caught up in the whole thing and leave out those closest to

44

you.

Sue:

We both thought we had better warn Jeremy about our selection, but could not get him on the telephone as he had gone to church. The second he entered the house the telephone went nonstop, and Jeremy is not someone who likes interviews and photographs, but he coped well. The worst thing in his eyes was that he got no gardening done that day! The best quote of all came from him in *The Birmingham Post:* 'my wife and daughter can survive Pole trek says solicitor!' We now had endless interviews, photographs and talks for a video.

One interesting but irritating fact that we learnt during our talks was when an interviewer, who had sat in on the selection, said graphology had played a significant part in the process. Mary Hadow is an expert, and when there was a difficult choice between two people, they went by the hand writing!- Huh - on my performance I was in the top three or four, but according to my handwriting I was at the bottom of the forty! I could remember writing some information about myself. I had written it out first, and then copied it, very neatly to begin with, and then in more and more of a hurry, which the graphologists said showed a lack of tenacity. Absolute rubbish, tenacity was my good point. Victoria was also written off at this stage due to her handwriting.

Victoria:

I have never felt so angry in my life. It almost left a bitter taste in my mouth after the euphoria of the day. How dare they make assumptions about my character based on my handwriting. Anyone who knows me

45

could have told them that a) I have totally illegible writing and b) I have various styles depending on my mood - a sure sign of schizophrenia!

Sue:

On to a pub lunch, and then the journey home. It was very awkward saying goodbye to those who had not been chosen, one minute they were team mates and next minute it was them and us. Victoria's mobile was going nonstop for interviews and we arrived back home to find a rather shell shocked Jeremy. However we were on such a high that we swept him along with us. It was champagne all round.

The next day we still had not come down to earth, there were more interviews with the BBC, and the newspapers. At the station I found it rather disconcerting to find myself on the front page of *The Birmingham Post*, half a page. I held *The Times* up in front of my face on the way to work in Birmingham. We had become media celebs overnight!

Edward had a bit of a shock when he was travelling home on the Gatwick Express, having just spent six weeks in Mexico. He opened up his *Times*, only to see, on page three, his mother and sister staring out at him. As he said, when you are feeling rather jet lagged and a bit grey, to see this and to read quotes such as: 'they were among the strongest, most courageous women I have ever met'! (Pen Hadow in *The Times*), and that: 'it's brilliant to be going with my mother, we'll make a great team', was all a bit much!   Not the sort of thing to see at seven in the morning having been on the 'redeye' flight. Some of the articles were very over the top but we had great entertainment reading them all.

We had a week of intensive interviews and still felt on a complete high. It was hard for Victoria as she had to rush off to Newcastle to run a careers course, but perhaps it helped to get her feet a bit more on the ground. One of the most cheering things was that so many friends were supportive in sending cards and letters of congratulation. At this stage we both thought - "Help" - but knowing that everyone was behind us meant a lot. Gradually life returned to normal and we both suddenly realised that now this was real and we would have to train seriously. But how?

The gym was the answer, but the problem was that neither of us are really natural gym people. Victoria found an excellent one in Putney, and I used my local leisure club, Patshull Park, for my training. At Patshull the staff were incredibly helpful and supportive and worked out programmes to boost my fitness levels. It was easier to push myself to go to the gym because now there was a purpose to it all. I also went circuit training in the village with Emma Pass every Wednesday evening, and again, she was marvellous at working out what should be done. Older bodies need a slightly different regime to those of Victoria's age!

Victoria:

I had an amazing coach at Putney Leisure Centre, Jon, who not only helped me to get fit but motivated me when I was feeling down after a long day at work. After ten hours of interviewing people and talking to clients on the phone, the last thing I wanted to do was go for a two hour workout in the gym. However thanks to Jon and my flatmate Zoe, I managed it most evenings.

Sue:

One of the first get-togethers we had was in London at a little

East End pub by Caroline's office in order to discuss fund raising. Obviously the whole expedition depended upon this, and as the empty glasses piled up the ideas became more outrageous, even to making a record - had they ever heard the two of us singing? In the end the choices were to sell postcards, to have a giant polar party and to all go out and find sponsors. Easier said than done.

My job was to arrange a group training weekend, which was organised to take place at Plas y Brenin, in Wales. We had this in November, and remarkably, we managed to get fourteen of the squad together, plus two leaders and Rosie's trainer Brian, who was very keen that we should all ridge run as part of the training. Had he seen the ridges on Snowdon? Especially as they were covered with snow. But it was a wonderful weekend, fantastic views, and the covering of snow and ice helped to make it all the more memorable. We did the Horseshoe on Snowdon on the Saturday and on Sunday climbed another peak, Tryffyn. Half way up, on a particularly steep bit, Jan suddenly said, 'it's Remembrance Day , I should be at the Cenotaph.' So we decided to stop for two minutes, one of the most moving Remembrance Days we have had. You could hear nothing except the wind blowing and a bird or two in the distance. The clouds were whisking across a sunny sky and we all felt this was a very special moment that would mean a lot to us. It was a successful weekend and very nice to find ourselves not in competition with each other. Before there had always been a slight feeling of having to prove yourself better than any one else.

Victoria:

By now we had a letter from Matty McNair, who was to be one

48

of our guides, giving us some ideas on training. She was, we felt, someone who was totally focussed on the north; the BBC had produced a documentary about her which we all watched avidly, as this was the woman with whom we would have to pass some time in difficult conditions. The statement that remained with us more than any others was that she did not like trees because they get in the way of the scenery. Some of her ideas were impossible, such as cross-country skiing, not having any snow on our back door steps, but others proved brilliant at improving fitness.

Sue:

The main training aid for the next four or five months was to be car tyres, three or four of them, attached to a waist harness, and dragged round fields and woodland, to the amusement of all passers by. Friends could always tell where I had been doing the pulling as all the paths were swept free of leaves and smoothed off! This is the sort of resistance training done by rugger players, we were a little concerned that we might end up with six-pack type abdominals, but luckily we did not.

Victoria:

I was a great Sunday afternoon entertainment in Richmond Park. People stopped and asked me what on earth I was doing, some even took photographs, but when we eventually arrived in Resolute Bay we found that pulling our Arctic sledges, all 150lbs of them, was no problem at all. You walked with ski sticks, and your pace, in order to simulate the Arctic, should not be more than about 1mph. It was very slow, and very hard work but incredibly fit-making. I never went anywhere without my tyres in the back of the car just in case there was an opportunity to practise. Mum took her bicycle with her as this was her favourite form of exercise. I sometimes ran back from the office, just off Piccadilly, to my flat in Putney, quite a run.

Sue:

We had some weekends arranged on Dartmoor, which we did in groups of four or five. I felt that from my point of view they were probably better for getting to know the others, and not necessarily for increasing fitness levels. We had all worked out the best way of training for ourselves and the Dartmoor weekends tended to give us a mental boost in seeing that we were all at much the same level.

By now Pen was beginning to get some sponsorship, but it was a struggle. Lucy Roberts was busy organising the Polar Party. St. John's Ambulance was proving a great help with this, providing office space and a mailing list. The problem was finding a venue, and getting things moving in a very short time, as we had to have most of the money in by the middle of January. As individuals we each had to put in £1,500. As neither of us had this money we decided that the easiest way to raise it was to treat the whole expedition as a sort of sponsored walk, so we wrote to every friend, acquaintance and local industrialist we could think of, telling them that after the initial £3,000 for our joint costs the rest would go to charity. We were staggered at just how generous our friends were. In the end we actually managed to give well in excess of £6,000 to various charities. It was quite incredible, and wonderful to know just how supportive our friends were.

As always those most difficult to interest in sponsorship were the larger local companies, with the exception of Tarmac, SJ.Dixon &

Son and GKN Technology who all contributed generously. You would have thought that local women doing something exciting would have perhaps inspired them into helping, but we thought that perhaps it was the woman thing again! Everyone wanted to know how we were doing, and we were beginning to find it somewhat embarrassing at parties when everyone wanted to know about the expedition. One plus from Victoria's point of view was that she did find the men clustered round her, she has never been such an attraction in her life - her polar groupies she calls them!

So Christmas came, suddenly it was 1997 and we were going to the Arctic THIS YEAR. It felt as if we were on a giant conveyor belt and nothing would stop this whole process. Time seemed to go quicker and quicker, and the first weekend in January we all had a compulsory training weekend in the Brecon Beacons. Everyone turned up and it was really good to see the whole team together for the first time. We had some wonderful walking, very snowy and bitterly cold in the evening, quite a problem hammering tent pegs into frozen ground. There was a shelter, a sort of bothy, where some of the others put down their bags, but as it was a hard stone floor the two of us and Lucy thought the tent would be better, which it definitely was. Especially when some TA people on exercise came in rather late, and having got over the shock of finding the bothy full of women, proceeded to have a party.

We were all cold in the night. Victoria woke up feeling dreadful, she had some sort of bug and in the end took a short cut back to the pub. But for the others, a last walk up to the top of the hill in the morning and then on to the pub for lunch and information on how things were going.

Victoria:

That makes me sound like a total wimp. I had in fact been very ill over Christmas and had not eaten or been outside for well over a week. However polar explorers have to fight on and I did not dare ring up Pen and say that I was ill. In retrospect I probably should have done.

Sue:

We were all hungry because of the exercise, but nervous, because this was the day that we would be given the dates and make up of the five teams; then everything would be real. Up to now it was all rather vague, a happening in the far distant future, but once we had dates there would be no escape. We were all called in to see Pen one by one, and were each asked for another £2,000, a large sum of money on top of the initial £1,500, but £3,500 for the adventure of a life time is not so much. We were not quite sure why he could not speak to us together, and tell us that the money was still short, but he had to give people the opportunity to back out if they felt they could not pay any more. As we had all put so much into the expedition and trained so hard, it would have been terrible to back out at this stage, in a way we would have lost face with our friends. In theory if this money could be raised, we would be reimbursed the £2,000, but most of us realised that we probably wouldn't see it again. (In the event, we actually did get back approximately £800.)

Having talked to us all, Pen showed us the suits we would be wearing. Very smart they looked too, we could all see ourselves skiing in them the next year, impressing our friends! Then, eventually, the teams and the dates. We were to be five teams of four, and I think that at that time everyone wanted to be in the final team. And would Victoria and I be together - were they going to split us up? The first team - Penguin Alpha - was announced: Ann Daniels, Claire Fletcher, Sue Fullilove and Jan McCormack. The second team - Penguin Bravo - was then announced: Rose Agnew, Karen Bradburn, Catherine Clubb and Emma Scott, but still no sign of us. Were we going together?

Then Penguin Charlie, and there we were, with us would be Lynne Clarke and Juliette May. The next team, Penguin Delta, was to consist of Andree Chadwick, Sarah Jones, Paula Power and Rosie Stancer. Finally, Penguin Echo was made up of Caroline Hamilton, Zoe Hudson, Pom Oliver and Lucy Roberts. Eventually Paula swapped with Juliette and joined us, as Juliette had problems with getting away at that time. We then had our dates, and there we were, team Charlie had to be fit and raring to go by 24th March, in under three months time.

Now it was time to raise more of the much needed money. This was the main problem; despite the injection of the extra £40,000 from the team members there was still a serious shortage of cash. So Lucy put huge quantities of energy into preparing for the Polar Party. Dawn French had agreed to be our Patron and to come to the party, she said that she had actually been selected, but had opted to stay at home and comfort the menfolk! Jeremy liked the idea of this and his one disappointment was that it never materialised! We all had to find enough items to auction, and eventually the party raised over £15,000, which was an incredible effort, and a great boost to the coffers.

Despite this the expedition was still on a knife edge financially, and we still had to find a fair bit of cash. Angela Mortimer plc., Victoria's firm, was generous and put in £10,000. Canadian Airlines were going to fly us all out for nothing, Bradstock would insure us, Damart clothing were very generous in giving us all our thermal gear, and also £10,000. Vander clothing gave us our outerwear, plus insulation from Carrington. Hollingsworths and Gills, both local companies, also helped us with food supplies for base camp. The generosity of people and their companies never ceased to amaze us. But we still needed more cash.

Then, a real shot in the arm, Penguin Biscuits came up with a major sponsorship deal, and suddenly we were the McVitie's Penguin Polar Relay. A mouthful in all senses of the word, as they were to give us all six biscuits a day per person for the expedition, and supply those of our families left at home. A wonderful publicity gimmick, the first penguins to get to the North Pole! The biggest bonus was that Penguin Biscuits do not freeze in extreme temperatures.

Victoria:

When I asked my boss, John Mortimer, to sponsor us I never imagined in my wildest dreams that he would be interested. I had only been with the company for two and a half years and was not a particularly senior member of the staff. However he came up trumps, much to my relief as the expedition would not have been possible without their kind donation.

Sue:

By now our training was becoming second nature. We had been told to put on weight, but with the exercise we were doing it was proving impossible. This was the ultimate diet. Two hours in the gym, then eat as much as you can as often as you can, and you still lose about one pound a week. The only problem was that it was quite hard work and very time consuming. I went training with Victoria one day, and it was rather a relief to find that she was really no fitter than me. This was always my worry, that I would let her down, and the other team members.

Every Sunday I tried to go for a sixteen mile run with the dogs. I had quite a good route, hardly any roads. My main problem was that the dogs got to know where all the interesting holes were, so I did spend some time occasionally lying on the ground screaming down them after the dogs. Rosie came to stay for a few days tyre pulling and we did the run. She was incredibly fit and extremely strong, despite being so small.

By mid March the Expedition had started and the first relay team was out on the ice. In general expeditions to the Pole cannot start before the beginning of March, when the sun first comes up. A clear hour of daylight has to be available for the pilot to drop the expedition onto the ocean. There is no one down on the ground to guide him in, or test the ice, so it has to be done visually, which can be quite a problem.

The first team set off on March 14th : Penguin Alpha. They were dropped just by Ward Hunt Island, a tiny blob north of Ellesmere Island. The whole expedition planned to walk along the 75th parallel of longitude, this was the shortest distance and the part of the ocean that, in theory, would have less drift and fewer currents (which can be a major problem sometimes). Alpha's main worry would be the massive pressure ridges which form as the sea ice is pushed against the unyielding mass of Ellesmere Island; some could be up to forty feet high.

Each team was to walk for approximately two to two and a half weeks and each successive team would, in theory, walk further than the preceding team as conditions improved. After their allotted time on the ice they would radio in their position and a weather report and hopefully the pilots would be able to fly out with the next team and do a swap, keeping the relay going. As the days lengthened each team would walk progressively longer hours and there would eventually be twenty four hours of daylight.

In theory, the whole expedition had to be finished by the end of May, as by then the ice has broken up to such a degree, due to the melting, that it is impossible to walk safely. It had been planned that as one team was flown onto the ice to walk, the next one would arrive and start their training. We were never to be in the Arctic all together, though we, as the middle team, met everyone else at some time when we were there. The fact that only the final team would reach the Pole was something that most of us could come to terms with quite easily. We were part of a team effort, and without each one of us they would not be able to arrive.

Victoria:

Things were now hotting up. We seemed to have interviews non stop, and in the middle of this I left my house in Putney. Jamie, my boyfriend, and I spent twenty four hours moving all my junk home much to Mum and Dad's horror. Where in the world would we store it? It is still in the stable one year later!

By this stage I was beginning to get fed up with all the interviews. Being an interviewee is just like being in a cattle market. You are herded into a studio, meet the journalist for approximately two minutes, talk live on air and then leave. The ones who were interested were usually journalists from the papers, such as Shirley Tart (*Wolverhampton Express and Star*) and Rosemary Carpenter

(Daily Express). Our favorite photographer was the man from *The Birmingham Post* - a great booming man who loved Katy (the dog!). The *Daily Express* photographer said 'come on girls, smile Sue, I know your sort' or 'OK Mum (to Gran) you need a hug'! We were pretty good at posing by now, mother leaning on daughter and vice versa. Smile, grit our teeth, pull the tyres, put on our white jackets, pose inside, pose outside, the photographer prefers not to have the sun so we must wait for a cloud even if it takes five minutes.

Gran (Dad's mother) arrived for a week's holiday in the middle of all this. We had thought that by the last week everything would have calmed down. It ended up being one of the most frenetic weeks ever, but enormous fun, and the three of us have never laughed so much. One of our interviews was at Pebble Mill, with Jenny Wilkes, live on Radio WM. Gran came along (called Nan by the people there), and we were slightly worried that she might say something during the interview, but luckily not! One always imagines rather smart radio studios, but quite the opposite, they are often scruffy and informal.

When we arrived home from the interview the door bell went and the tractor driver from the field opposite was standing there. He had heard us on the radio in his tractor cab, seen us arrive and wanted to wish us good luck. This was something that would never cease to amaze us. People who we had never met would come up to us or even find our number in the telephone directory and say that they were thinking of us. We are too often too cynical about the human race, and this certainly helped restore my faith in humanity.

On Wednesday a charming woman, Rosemary Carpenter, came down from the *Daily Express* to interview us. We were now having problems with the publicity. The papers wanted the interviews, but the Polar Travel Company wanted cash from them for the expedition. We both felt like pigs in the middle, wanting to be helpful to both sides! We had the usual photographs of us pulling car tyres up and down the field, the dogs being very unhusky like and running up and down behind us. Rosemary departed, the telephone rang, and this time it was an interview with *The Express and Star*, given while Mum was heating the soup for lunch! *The Express and Star* had been very helpful the whole way through, both with interviews and by giving us free camera films, with no obligation what-soever. Next stop was an interview with Cable Television, again with Gran, who by now knew all the answers we gave and we reckoned that she could do the interviews for us! She seemed to enjoy it all thoroughly.

Sue:

Philip and Ed said their worst problem is that all their friends think they are wimps with a mum and a sister going off to the Pole and them staying at home!

Victoria:

I had a hectic day on the Thursday before we left for Resolute Bay, as I had to catch the train up to London in order to meet the BBC and Caroline Hamilton. All the car parks were full (Prince Charles was visiting Wolverhampton and the multi storey car park had collapsed), so it was a total nightmare. I missed the first train and in the end left my car in the short stay park (twenty minutes maximum), and hoped for the best. I finally arrived in London and headed off to the BBC to learn how to use a tape machine which we would use to record a daily diary for

Radio 4. It was then a mad rush across London, calling in on various friends en route to say goodbye, all rather emotional.

Once at Caroline's we got to see a fantastic video sent from Base Camp at Resolute. We could not believe it, everything looked so comfortable - running water and heating. We could not let on to all our friends as they all thought we were going to be training in some inhospitable outback - we had thought that as well. We then spoke to Penguin Bravo who were already up there and got lots of helpful hints on what to take up with us - from food, to clothing to Tampax (very expensive apparently). Watching the video really did bring it all home, only four days left. We were starting to lose that confident feeling and the nerves were showing. However, seeing Paula was helpful, as it reinforced my belief that we had a great team and we could get through anything - a good team is all important. Sitting on the train to Wolverhampton that evening, wondering if my car would have been towed away, I was made aware that there are far more important things in life than walking to the North Pole. I sat next to a group of four pensioners from Wolverhampton discussing for thirty minutes if you can turn left or right at the junction at Chapel Ash!! The things that make the world go round.

By Friday I was starting to get a little stressed - mainly because Mum was showing no nerves and was in her usual laid back mood. It made it far worse for me as I felt really pathetic feeling nervous. Dad seemed all right, even though he was very worried he did not like to show it. BBC *Midlands Today* rang up and asked if they could come and film us, they threatened to do it when we were in church on Sunday, but we thought that might be the last straw for Dad!

Sue:

At this stage I still felt as if it were someone else going on the expedition, not me. Victoria was definitely very scratchy and you had to tread carefully with her. I spent most of the last week filling the freezer for Jeremy but everyone felt so sorry for him that they asked him out nearly every night and nothing was eaten. By now I just wanted to get on with it, I had paid every bill, answered every letter and had bought enough dog food for six weeks, I found myself trying to fill the time in order to make Monday arrive more quickly!

Victoria:

On Saturday we all went out to a marvellous family supper as by now the boys were both at home. It was a typical family supper with lots of gentle arguing, as there often is when everyone is together, but also partly because of nervousness. You could feel the tension mounting, particularly with what was not said. No one liked to say any 'what ifs'.

We all went to the Palm Sunday service, my favourite. It was very embarrassing, as apart from being prayed for in the intercessions, the vicaress asked both Mum and me to come up to the front of the church at the end and tell the congregation what we were doing, why and how we felt. This was followed by prayers for us. Although embarrassed we were also very touched. *Midlands Today* were waiting for us when we got back, so yet again, on with the tyres for the last time, marvellous, then upstairs to film us packing. So there we were: one interviewer, one camera man, one brother on a bed, videoing the proceedings, while Mum and I made rather forced conversation to each other, discussing what we

60

were packing. Apparently when this interview was eventually shown on television it appeared that we were in a bathroom, as all you could see in the spare room apart from us was the washbasin! Philip's film of the proceedings came out well, and could be used in the ultimate documentary!

Sunday evening turned out to be relatively quiet as all the phone calls had stopped by eight, much to Dad's relief as he hates the phone at the best of times. He felt that during the previous week it had totally disrupted any conversation or meal, and had completely governed our lives. I suddenly realised how much I was going to miss my friends. We were not going for that long, but all the build up had made it seem like such a major adventure. My flatmate, Zoë, and I tended to speak most days and as (according to her father) we cannot even change a pair of knickers without consulting each other, life was going to be difficult over the next two months!

Sue:

It was rather a stressful supper, then there we were, packed up and ready to go. Jeremy complained that I fidgeted in bed all night, was it worry?

Victoria:

I did not sleep at all, thanks to nightmares about polar bears, and then just as I finally dropped off I was woken up by Tessa (the dog) licking me! When I woke up it was Monday 24th March D-DAY! We got up feeling very nervous but made ourselves eat breakfast, and set off for the airport with the boys following in their car. There was dreadful traffic but we arrived at Heathrow in plenty of time and collected our tickets. Pam Callaghan was there, she is a most efficient PR person but she did keep asking us who we had been interviewed by, and wanted all our thoughts and opinions as we were checking in. We were obviously nervous, and wanted to spend time with the family, which made it quite hard.

Lynne Clarke caught up with us, having flown down from Manchester. Serena Chance from the Polar Travel Company turned up with 80 kgs of salami (Canadian Airlines seemed slightly surprised, but it was part of our rations, that we had to take with us), and the rest of our kit, which we had to pack at the check in desk. My hand luggage weighed a ton - Easter eggs for the boys at Base Camp and two bottles of Moet et Chandon from Henny Frazer. Caroline arrived on her bike, manic as ever, with pressies for us all! We unwrapped them later and found they were mini books, each containing two Winnie the Pooh stories!

By this stage we had all checked in and it was time to go. There was that dreadful awkward silence when there is something in the back of all our minds, but it was left unsaid. Would Dad and the boys see us again? We were much less worried than them, but you could see them thinking it. I was very tearful when it came to saying goodbye. I am not good at good byes at the best of times, but the boys took great delight in winding me up! I was also worried about Dad being on his own; he had a few tears in his eyes but seemed to be all right.

Then we were off. In that split second all the nerves went and we were really, really excited. So we left the men, and feeling in need of a pick me up, sat down to have a quick beer and a chat. Suddenly we heard over the tannoy a call for the last remaining passengers on the

Canadian Airlines flight to Toronto. However we had our priorities right and having downed our drinks we shot off to Duty Free and only then to the departure gate! Imagine if we had missed the flight. It would have been a disaster to be stuck at Heathrow at this stage. We could all see the headlines - would-be Arctic explorers get lost at Heathrow!

Sue:

This was the worst moment, Jeremy stood there, looking very alone and very forlorn, despite having Philip and Ed standing one on each side. Victoria did not help matters by getting rather emotional. The only thing to do was to go through into the departure lounge as quickly as possible, but it was a dreadful five minutes. I felt very guilty at leaving him.

Victoria:

A Canadian came up to me while we were having our beer, and said he had seen me on CBC, in Toronto. They knew all about the expedition. We began to realise that there was international interest and it was a funny feeling.

It was a good flight. Now that we had become celebs we got to visit the cockpit! Looking down at Labrador we suddenly realised what we were doing. A landscape made up of snow, ice and trees and it would be even more desolate at Resolute. We saw the St. Lawrence Seaway, which was totally frozen. Canada from the coast to Toronto really did look very cold and uninviting. We wondered what we were doing, but it was all happening now and we were being swept along with the tide. It was too late to back out.

DISASTER! We arrived in Toronto and went to pick up all our luggage, but in true Victoria fashion the one bit of luggage which had all our Vander stuff in it, i.e. all the cold weather clothing, was missing. I unfortunately caused a bit of a fuss when I found that it had not even been put on the plane. They had realised straight away, (a fax had been sent from Heathrow to say it was there when we were still in the air), so why couldn't they put it on the next flight which was only two hours later? I just could not understand it.

A really nice man eventually caught up with us in the departure lounge for Edmonton, and said that he had arranged for it to go via Ottawa and Frobisher Bay, and arrive in Resolute on Thursday. I felt this was a bad omen and had no faith that it would ever get there. It turned out this had also happened with some of both Alpha's and Bravo's luggage.

We managed to get the salami through customs quite easily; the agricultural customs officer had come from Kidderminster twenty years ago! We met up with Sue Self, the reserve, at the check-in desk for Edmonton. She was on very good form. Since the four of us had already bonded, we just hoped that she would fit in. I think that it was probably quite difficult for her. So now it was on with the next flight. It had been seven hours to Toronto, and was now five hours on to Edmonton.

Sue:

Victoria got quite stressed and angry, and felt she should not have done. She was probably tired after the long journey and was feeling extremely nervous, but there was nothing you could do. I felt you just had to go with the flow!

Victoria:

We were put up for the night in Edmonton in a real Thelma and Louise motel. A truckers halt but very adequate. The truckers' refrigerated vans were running the whole night long. It was a totally bare, barren and windswept place. Sitting in our rooms watching the Oscars on television was a surreal experience, but by this time it was 10.30 pm Edmonton time which meant 5.30 am UK time, i.e. we had been up for nearly twenty four hours so were shattered.

Lynne meanwhile had decided to try on her sledging suit only to discover a major problem, it did not fit, panic! She then realised with much amusement that she had put her leg in the arm hole and now could not get it out. It needed a lot of brute force from Paula to get it unstuck!

In the cafe the next morning sat the truckers, all men and all wearing their baseball caps, their vast lorries left running while they came in and had breakfast. The whole restaurant hushed as the five of us walked in. Total silence. This was to become quite a common experience as not surprisingly the Arctic is very much a man's world.

We had a fantastic breakfast with massive door steps of eggy bread (french toast), bacon and orange juice. We were starving, and it was perfect. We wanted anything to eat except chicken, which is apparently the only food served on Canadian Airlines.

Mum and I went into 'Downtown Le Duc'. It really was quite unlike anything we had ever seen before. There are endless vast buildings in the middle of nowhere and everywhere was white, not a clean white but a slushy, mucky white. The adverts in the papers are all for special value weedkiller or special offer wheat, no sign of any international company. Everyone has a truck and wears a cap or hat. It seems to be almost impersonal - no comforts or family atmosphere. But in reality it is quite the opposite: everyone knows everyone, and there is a real community spirit.

The liquor store was shut, but luckily we could get some beer in the airport. Very important as Resolute Bay is dry and all would-be explorers need alcohol whilst training! By this stage we had twenty four pieces of baggage between us. In the departure lounge a woman came up to us. She worked with young offenders and had read about us, and asked if we could autograph her book as a sign of what they could achieve? By now we were getting used to people recognising us - admittedly five women in white coats did rather stand out in a crowd - and while we found it embarrassing at times, we also felt very proud and privileged to be part of a unique British expedition.

But more than anything else we felt both elated and apprehensive, a real mixture of excitement and collywobbles, about the adventure and the unknown challenges that were getting closer and closer.

Chapter Four

Resolute Bay

Victoria:

We finally got on the plane to Resolute, it was half full of passengers (in the back) and half full of freight (in the front), including all the supplies for Resolute, plus all our stuff - we hoped! We were convinced it would be nose heavy when taking off. Seeing the plane fitted with skis suddenly brought home to us where we were going. Edmonton may seem cold, but at least it had real runways and a normal way of life. We were now heading north of the Arctic Circle, into the big unknown.

There were about forty passengers on board: quite a few Inuit (Eskimos) all wearing blue parkas with fur ruffs on their hoods, some sponsors from Holland going out to support the Dutch expedition which was on the ice, plus all the guys who worked up at the Polaris mine, which is about 200 miles from Resolute. I sat next to a man from New Zealand who had sold his farm for a great deal of money and, having always dreamed of going to the North Pole, was coming up for a two week holiday. At the time I thought he must be crazy, but now I can totally empathise.

As we approached Yellowknife, the landscape was flat - lakes, trees and nothing, quite desolate. We felt like medieval flat earth explorers, about to drop off the edge of the world. When we landed it was -21⁰C - quite cold, but sunny. It seemed a fairly large place.

As we were taking a photograph, a man came up and offered to do it for us. It turned out that he was the Air Traffic Controller, and originally came from Newcastle on Tyne. He then gave us a guided tour of the control tower, all this during a twenty minute stopover. We began to panic as we could see ourselves missing the plane, but he assured us that it could not take off without us, as he was in charge! It was slightly depressing as we left Yellowknife, because we realised Dad was watching the Nine O'Clock News for the second time, and we still had not arrived.

Our next stop was Cambridge Bay. Nothing. A snow and gravel runway, and a few huts in the distance, the smallest terminal imaginable. It was sunny, but getting colder -25^{0}C, and the wind was blowing. A scene of desolation. It was like every book that we had read about the Arctic. It was the idea of sheer survival. Everything, even the aeroplanes, were half buried under a snowy landscape which disappeared into the horizon. But when we met the pilot he seemed very relaxed. As the plane only came twice a week for deliveries, it was a social occasion.

After a twenty minute stop we were on the move again, the snow all whipped up as the plane took off. We were quite relieved not to have another aeroplane meal, just snacks this time, and the inevitable Mars bar for tea. Announcements were now made in Inuit as well as French and English. Looking out of the window it was hard to tell whether it was cloud or land we were looking at, as they blended into one another.

It was all so beautiful: the sun and shadows, ridges and cracks in the ice and Somerset Island in the distance. There were no trees now, and nothing to fix your eye on to give you any idea of distance or scale. At some time we must have crossed the frozen North West Passage, but there was no sign of any navigable channel. We were starting to think what we were doing, it was getting closer all the time.

Seven hours after leaving Edmonton we landed at Resolute. There was no runway, just a marked snow strip, and you wondered how the pilots ever landed. You could be in the north of Scotland, but it was intensely cold: - 29°C.

Sue:

We were met by Nobby and Mike. It was good to see them, and it was as if we had finally reached home. They were the Polar Travel Company organisers at the base camp. Pen Hadow was there, on and off, as he had various other expeditions to lead. Nobby was in reality Peter Noble-Jones, a chartered surveyor by profession, who had taken some time out to travel and had been persuaded to help out at Base Camp. Mike Ewart- Smith, sometimes known as Goldie, was a venture capitalist and a keen sailor, a Cowes champion, who had also been persuaded that the Arctic was preferable to London. They were wonderful, organising the rations, equipment, radio communications and, much to our amazement, the sewing and mending of clothes - an enjoyable role reversal for us.

Resolute Bay really was exactly like you see in the photographs, a tiny terminal building with giant icicles hanging off the roof. In the distance we could see just a few huts, covered in snow. We gathered up our luggage, the quantity of which seemed to have grown every time we came to collect it, and by now we also had a couple of bunches of flowers, a present for our unknown hosts. Flowers are the most wonderful luxury in the Arctic. In a world of white anything with colour is appreciated, the only problem being that they don't last long. We put our equipment into the truck, which was driven across to the Rookery, named because of the fact that we were the Penguin Relay, and being birds.... It was a shack, well, actually, a garage. We left the terminal and walked over. It was so cold that the hairs in your nostrils froze, a dry cold so intense you could feel it chilling your body, and very quickly too. We had not yet put on our Arctic gear, as it was still at Heathrow.

Victoria:

We had all gone quiet. The enormity of what we were letting ourselves in for had suddenly hit home. We were in a totally alien environment. Nothing can prepare you for the culture shock, and the intense cold was just numbing.

Sue:

The airport was very much the 'white' community - government workers, airport personnel and those from the Polaris mine. Everyone knows everyone, and everyone is a friend of everyone else. About five kilometres away there is Resolute Bay itself, the Inuit community, a small village of only a hundred residents. Well, there were until the week before, when a love triangle went wrong and one man killed the other two. There were now ninety eight inhabitants. The court only comes every six months and after it finishes the sitting there are often two or three people missing, as they have been found guilty. Most locals now realise that trial by jury is the best - it is virtually impossible to find an independent jury up there as everyone is related. Once a tourist was actually roped in to be a member of a jury!

The hut where we were staying was a two minute walk from the airport. There were only about ten houses/huts in this part of Resolute.

70

All were extremely well heated - too hot! Base Camp adjoined the house of a couple called Gary and Diane. It was once their garage and was now converted by us to have three or four rooms. Two 'bedroom' areas, a computer room, somewhere to sit and a store area, which included a loo that, instead of flushing by water, flushed by fire. I felt very wary about using it; I was vindicated because it suddenly went wrong and the hut was full of smoke and bits of, well, I did not like to think what, and we never used it again!

Our senses were being overloaded with differing impressions. We were not going to be in the house rented for training, as we had actually arrived a week early owing to Canadian Airlines not wanting to fly us during Easter weekend. Gary and Diane were a wonderful warm and friendly couple who used to live in Sudbury, Ontario. They had moved up to Resolute for a two year posting (it is very good money) and were still there six years later. We slept in their house for two nights with the luxury of showers, totally unexpected, but we did find it difficult to get used to the incredible heat of the houses. The heating is never turned off, night or day, summer or winter, so you spend the whole time taking clothes on and off even if you slip outside for a couple of minutes. Such as when Diane fed two Arctic hares every day, just outside her front door, virtually the only wildlife that we saw. Apparently the temperature never exceeds 10^0C. It is very expensive to live here, the water costs \$2,000 a month which is paid for by the Government, and the house rental is \$600 a month. The whole region is very heavily subsidised by the State.

Having been introduced to Gary and Diane, we were then whisked off to No 75 - the training house - as Penguin Bravo were out for the night on the ice. We watched a video of Alan Bywater. Alan was a twenty one year old British/Canadian who attempted to go solo but did not last very long. He fell in, hauled himself out, and was rescued by David Hempleman-Adams (going unsupported to North Pole with the Norwegian Rune Gjeldnes). David was worried that the rescue would delay his expedition and could cause it to fail - no outside aid must be given to an unsupported expedition.

Mike and Nobby cooked us dinner, as by now we were all feeling rather jet lagged. Driving back from the Inuit village to the top village we felt so cold - there was no time to heat the vehicle in the short five kilometre journey, so we were chilled to the bone. However we quickly became accustomed to the cold. Within one week we could walk around without too much protection on our faces. It still meant wearing balaclavas and scarves, but not quite so many layers!

When we got back to the Rookery it was time for Penguin Alpha to radio in. Having last seen them in the warmth of the UK it was a strange feeling, hearing their crackling voices across the airwaves. We were only allowed half an hour of radio time, as the airways are used by the other teams on the ice, and also the aircraft themselves. As we went to bed that evening we saw the Hale-Bopp comet, one of the last opportunities to see it because each day gets longer by twenty minutes, and soon there would be twenty four hours daylight. Our first Arctic sunset was stunning, a wonderful turquoise sky with the sea ice changing colour as the sun went down. Somehow you forget that it is ice.

Resolute started life as an air base, but because of worries about the sovereignty of the North West Territories (due to the cold war and the proximity to Russia), Inuit people were brought in from Quebec and expected to fend for themselves with the help of government subsidies.

They were used to a totally different environment where there were trees and no dark season, We felt it must be a very numbing life as all there is to do is husky racing, polar bear and musk-ox hunting, or eating raw meat, which is even better if slightly off! We did feel concerned about the lack of educational opportunities; if anyone wanted further education they had to leave home and go south.

Ice Mice is what the people of Resolute called all the hopeful polar explorers who turned up each spring. They would come for a few days, train and set off, then that is another expedition on its way. Apparently all the inhabitants of Resolute thought that we were just a bunch of women who had no chance of making it to the Pole, but by the time our team arrived they were starting to believe in us. We all felt that the Penguin Relay must make it just to prove everyone wrong. By the end we were odds on favourite to make it to the Pole, even though the odds are normally four to one against an expedition getting there. The Arctic world is a very small one - there is a community of polar travellers, everyone knows of everyone else, especially we polar women as we stood out in our red gear. Most other expeditions are transitory, but because we kept changing over and some of us were always present, the local men seemed to be fascinated.

The next day, 26th March, we spent most of the time packing supplies for Penguin Bravo. It was important to weigh everything precisely as every gram would count when you were pulling it behind you. The quantity of food required surprised us, and when preparing it you had to take everything out of the wrappers so that fumbly fingers in the cold could eat without struggling. (Appendix 1.) We had 6,000 calories a day, the most that a human body can absorb in twenty four

73

hours.

Bravo came back from their three days on the ice, their final training session before the real thing. They were very focussed and though excited were obviously nervous. Up until this point our greatest fear had been being so cold in bed that you were unable to sleep, but much to our relief they assured us that this was rarely the case. One very important piece of advice that they gave us was to always be open with each other as the Arctic is not the place to have a falling out. It can be a life or death situation and you need to be working as a team.

Victoria:

One worrying piece of news was that the pill/Depro injections that we took to postpone our periods were not working; seemingly the Arctic was not a place for women. We would just have to learn to adapt.

Sue:

We rang home after lunch, as there were birthdays to wish well for and Jeremy to reassure. Apparently Tessa (the dog) was missing Victoria! It was strange to hear them so clearly when we already felt we were in a different world. Victoria and I were both lent some spare kit in order to keep us warm until our own suitcases arrived, and we were all given our Sorel boots, which we would wear constantly from then onwards. They were extremely comfortable; to begin with they felt enormous, but it was important to be able to wear several layers of socks. They had thick felt inner liners, coated in a foil layer for insulation, but were not waterproof as we were not expecting to go paddling in the Arctic Ocean. These boots were incredible and never caused any team

74

member any problems; no one had blisters, despite all the walking. Before they were invented, in the 1920's, explorers had to wear sealskin boots and as no moisture from sweaty feet could escape, the answer was to push in as much dry grass as possible to absorb the sweat - most uncomfortable!

We went off to explore the Inuit hamlet, and to help Mike buy food at the Co-op. This was to become, surely, the most expensive shopping trip in history; approximately £25 for twelve cans of coke and ten post cards! Unbelievable. We immediately understood why the majority of supplies were brought up from Edmonton and Yellowknife on the twice weekly flights.

We set out for a walk and went across the bay, literally! It was a very strange feeling the first time you were on sea ice. So, here we were, on the edge of the Arctic Ocean - but what *is* the Arctic Ocean. It's the smallest ocean there is, and some scientists even think that it is just part of the Atlantic rather than a real ocean, and call it the Arctic Sea. It was named by the ancient Greeks after Arktos, the bear, for a constellation in the northern skies.

It is a bitterly cold region, and in the winter the sun never rises and during the summer the sun never sets. It was too late for us to see the northern lights, but we did have wonderful sunsets. It has very little actual precipitation, about two inches a year so is dryer than the Sahara, but you can get a lot of sea mist.

The sea ice forms when the water temperature drops to -2^0C, instead of the more normal 0^0C, this is because of the salinity of the water. On average the pack ice does not exceed two metres in thickness, but about 70% of the ice never melts and can sometimes be as thick as fifty metres. This is multi-year ice, which is what we would always try to camp on, but there is also about 10% of the ocean that never freezes in the winter. You can meet giant icebergs which have broken off glaciers and in the winter they are frozen into the pack ice. There are tides, but with very little rise and fall, perhaps because there are so many islands. There is a fear that with global warming the Arctic ice cap could be reduced, so there were a number of scientists in the region to check the depth and measure drift. There were some quite strong currents, which we hoped we would not get swept into!

When we were on the ice in the bay we saw two boats frozen in - they had just been left there for the winter. There were also some very large wooden sledges just sitting on the ice. They were called Kamatiks - the Inuit word for sledge. Everything seemed very casual, but there was no one to walk off with anything. We came upon lots of patches where huskies had obviously been, Paula and Lynne found two of them tethered right against two dead ones - horrible.

The Inuit are very harsh to the dogs, they do not feed them much and let them lie there. If they survive then well and good, and if not it is just nature. It seemed dreadful and cruel to us but we cannot really interfere as it is a totally different culture. Strangely enough some looked quite warm and happy and were chewing on great bones with meat on them (we later discovered these were polar bear thighs).

We walked along for a couple of hours, and during one brief stop Lynne 'Paco' Clarke taught us the flamenco. It was a bit of a problem doing it as we were wearing the very large chunky boots, but we learnt the basics! To this day we are not entirely sure what brought on this sudden desire for dancing the flamenco, it must have looked a very strange sight. Ice madness perhaps.

Victoria:

Whenever I see the flamenco from now onwards I will always think about the North Pole!

Sue:

The ice had cracks in it, very deep, and as you walked there were different noises. Sometimes it echoed, sometimes it sounded like a dog growling or something being squeaked, every step made a different sound. There was no sense of distance, you could see some islands maybe two or three miles away, but they were actually twenty or thirty miles distant. The snow makes you lose all sense of perspective. You could see the waves, as if they had frozen instantly in mid break. The sun seemed to have a double halo round it and did not appear to go down at all quickly, despite it being dusk. At home it seems to drop so quickly, but at Resolute even at the end of March it was still fairly light at 9.30 pm.

We were hoping that Penguin Alpha would radio in during the evening. The back up communication was done by ARGOS, an emergency locator or signalling beacon. It used satellites, which sent signals to a US base in Maryland, who then e-mailed us at base camp with the position and messages. A list of coded messages was worked out, and every evening a number was set on the black box that is the ARGOS beacon. (Appendix 2.) Eventually we heard at about 9.00pm that communication was very poor, they were obviously having a problem with the radio. Again, this brought home to us the importance of communications, and that the people at Base Camp were just as

77

important as those on the ice.

We finished packing the food, and Victoria and Paula helped do the update on our Website. We had won the 'World Website of the Week', as there was a considerable amount of interest in our expedition, particularly in North America. It was sad that this was not so in the UK. The Russians had apparently e-mailed in to say that they had heard we were eating a lot of penguins, and they would be very interested in buying the skins! We went over to Diane and Gary's house to do all the repairs or changes needed for our kit, a real 'stitch and bitch' session! We had long talks about our families. Lynne was thirty seven, married to Ally with two children - Jack and Sam. She and Ally met at college and were surveyors up in Cheshire. She has a great sense of humour and is very down to earth. Paula was twenty nine and had spent the last six or seven years travelling, a definite nomad at heart. Sue Self was in her mid thirties, has a young son called Jamie, and lives with her partner up in Newcastle. It was a rather surreal feeling sitting in the Arctic, in a comfortable sitting room with heating and cups of tea, not at all what we had expected. Diane and Gary kept blowing in, Diane enjoying this unexpected female company. Resolute was male dominated, women were a rarity, especially four new ones every two weeks!

Victoria:

Later on while in the Rookery we discovered 'Channel 12' which all the men in Resolute watch. Surprise, surprise it was a porn channel, but not remotely sexy, just very funny! The only programmes on TV are the porn channel, the Antiques Roadshow, Coronation Street and the Labrador Games. A quite amazing programme, the Labrador Games. It appears to be made by amateurs with videos and consists of such exciting races as jumping over school benches with both feet together, or seal kicking, aiming at a piece of seal dangling from the roof. Or there were ski races, but not as we know them, in these you had to stop at some stage, light a fire, cook a meal, eat it and then ski off. The winners collect their medals while standing on old milk crates, rather wobbly sometimes. It did keep us very entertained, and perhaps during the long winter nights there is not much else to occupy your time apart from getting fit for the next event.

It was great being with Mum! We obviously bicker at times but generally get on extremely well, and we now had so much time to reminisce or exchange stories, something which one rarely has time to do in normal every day life.

Sue:

Having had all this hard work in a super heated house we felt in need of fresh air and exercise, Victoria's training as my daughter coming out. All three of my children say they still feel guilty if they don't have some form of exercise in the afternoon, though Edward fights hard to overcome this problem. So, having persuaded the others that air was what we needed, in the afternoon we walked up Martyrs Hill. Distances are very deceptive. It took a lot longer than we had imagined, and when we got there we were well above the bay. You could almost see the frozen sea moving with all the different shades of ice. The setting sun yet again was wonderfully photogenic and we were in danger of finishing our films before even starting out! We had taken toboggans with us, but they were not successful as the snow was too dry and the temperature too cold. It was becoming much colder now, especially when walking, mainly because of the wind, and Lynne had problems with her glasses freezing up. The wind chill really did make quite a difference.

Victoria:

As usual Mum and Sue Self had woken up early and started chatting. I did get really annoyed at them both waking up at an ungodly hour, as this was supposedly my holiday! I began to wonder why I was actually doing this. It was not fun and extremely cold. When we went out our eyelashes froze in seconds, and everything else including your hair was frozen, and that was after only an hour and a half.

Sue:

It was now time for Penguin Bravo to be going, but it was on and off, on and off. Originally it was hoped that they might share a flight with the Dutch team when it was being resupplied, but this was not going to happen. They did not want the resupply quite yet, so our team had to wait for a plane to be free. It was very difficult for Penguin Alpha, as their radio was not working, so there was no way we could tell them that the changeover has been postponed. They were probably waiting and wondering where we were. The worst was that they were only two miles from the 84th parallel, and they could not start walking again in case the changeover was suddenly brought forward. Everyone was sitting round waiting, rather tense, not settling to anything, and poor Bravo were on tenterhooks.

Geoff Somers came and introduced himself to us. He had worked for the British Antarctic Survey for years. He was one of the leaders of the Prince's Trust Magnetic North Pole Trip in 1996, and also had done the only longwise crossing of Antarctica by dog and sledge, the Trans-Antarctica Expedition of 1989/1990 - which would be the first and last with dogs. He was incredibly well travelled in the polar regions and was a quiet man, very private, he kept himself to himself. As we got to know him during the training we discovered what a fascinating, well read man he was, with the most varied selection of hidden talents He can juggle, he does wonderful tapestry, he is a good cook, has a very laid back sense of humour, and at the same time he can cope with being down in Antarctica for thirty months or so on end. He is also a proficient carpenter, and helped set up the SnowSled company, who provided our sledges. An amazing man, whom we quickly learned to trust.

Resolute was a place of wonderful freedom, you could be who or what you wanted. It did not matter how you appeared or where you came from, what mattered was what you were like as a person. We all felt almost as if we had been reborn as Arctic Explorers, happy with how we were and very much at peace with ourselves. It was a time to take stock of what you wanted out of life because all worries about work, finance or other problems seemed to disappear. Our only problems were the immediate ones of the expedition, but as a team we all felt the same so they all became smaller.

Victoria:

We realised that Dad would have no worries if he met Geoff and listened to him, I thought that he was not dissimilar to Dad. Mike was a funny character. A massive man, 6'6"! Quite shy and very bashful when around women, he was almost in his own world sometimes. We had spent many hours wondering who Nobby reminded us of, and a flash of inspiration, it was Baldrick from *Blackadder*. He was slightly less bashful when with us.

Both of them were typical bachelors with hair that stands up in the morning, and a room so messy you never dared walk into it! To top it off, rather than put on clean clothes each day they just turned their boxer shorts or shirts inside out and started again. Often a piece of clothing would be worn for two weeks or longer!! Both of them were to play a very important part in our lives whilst training, we came to rely on them totally, and the expedition could never have happened without them.

My luggage had arrived the day before, miraculously! It was marvellous to have our proper cold weather gear with us as well as the rest of the kit. The best thing was my banoffi mixture which I had carefully cooked back home. It tasted like heaven.

Sue:

Our first Friday was a marvellous day, we skidooed (snowmobiled) to Crystal City, an Arctic training camp, with three of the locals, Rick, Rick and Al. Everyone seemed to have the same name, but it made it a lot easier to remember. As we were five and there were only four skidoos, the men attached a box-like contraption to the back of one machine, into which two of us were put, with a duvet on top. Lynne and Victoria were first in the box, they looked very regal, like the snow queen, but only for the first few minutes. After that it was a matter of hanging on for grim death.

We drove through a winding valley, unbelievably stunning - it went on for ever, snow carved into ever more fantastic shapes by the wind, great drifts hanging off the sides, where the sun hit the drifts they seemed to sparkle. The only wildlife we saw was one lone raven, not surprising considering the noise the machines made. We had changed places and by now I was in the box, facing back, which was good because during the initial roar out of Resolute my goggles had completely steamed up and I could see nothing, which was perhaps not a bad thing! It was bitterly cold, -34^0C, especially when driving.

After we came out of the valley onto a big plain, we roared up to the top of a hill where we had the full impact of the view. The headlands, the sea, which you could almost see moving; a scene of total desolation. No habitation, no trees, just stony earth pushing its way up through the very thin layer of snow, most of which had been blown away in the wind. This was the sort of country that the musk-ox survived in.

Every time we stopped, the men had yet another swig of vodka! What they really liked was us hanging on for grim death, thighs tight against theirs, arms round their waists, our breasts tight into their backs, and our heads against theirs on their shoulders. Victoria disappeared at one stage, she and her driver suddenly drove off into the distance. I wondered whether I should follow her! Then we went down to the ocean, over the beach, over some ridges, as if the last two breakers had frozen, up and over, up and over, then onto the ocean. You could see the shore line, but the petrified breakers were incredible. Victoria had to pee, using her back zip for the first time, and it worked - no splash back. When he wanted to do the same thing Al was very discreet, and went back up the hill.

Victoria:

I was very embarrassed at this as none of us had attempted it before, but nature called. It was quite a complicated procedure the first time, as I had to master undoing a zip that stretched from my back to my belly button, a crap flap, while simultaneously checking the wind direction and trying not to appear awkward in front of four fascinated men!

Sue:

We then took over, which was a good thing as the vodka was starting to take effect. I drove back through the gorge, stunning, quite one of the most exhilarating fifteen minutes I think I have ever had. The others were on the hill above, and in the setting sun looked just like E.T. with the box trailing behind. We went back to the Rookery feeling totally on a high. Every day would bring some new happening so far removed from our lives at home that it seemed unreal. Perhaps if we were real explorers all this would be commonplace, but it was the unknown and the unusual that made it all such an adventure. I felt that for me the whole Resolute scene so far was rather like a reversion to childhood, I was finding new experiences and new pleasures, which made me feel I was in a whole new unreal world. It was very uplifting to have the opportunity to do something like this, at fifty something, when a lot of my acquaintances were perhaps wondering where they were going.

We were extremely cold on our return and a hot shower only just thawed out our hands. Then to bed, what a day. On the way there, each evening, I stood on the doorstep at 11.00 pm and looked at the pink streak in the sky to the north. Hale-Bopp was still there. Total silence. It was so peaceful standing on my own after a day with the others. All you could see were the hills, valleys and the sea, always the dominant feature. It put you into another world from home. The immensity of the sunset thrilled me every evening.

One of the other teams on the ice was 'Polar Free'. (Appendix 3.) They had helped Penguin Alpha by lending a battery (this had been the problem with their communications, a damaged battery, and was the reason they had not radioed in). Alpha had had quite a difficult time with the radio not working, but incredibly, when in their tent they had heard footsteps outside. Thinking it might be polar bears they looked out tentatively, and discovered it was the team from Polar Free! Both teams were delighted to see one other, as the chances of bumping into anyone else are pretty remote. Now that Alpha were in contact again, base camp could radio them to say that if they wanted to they could walk the last two miles to the 84th parallel while we tracked them on the ARGOS.

During this final radio transmission a changeover date was arranged and eventually Penguin Bravo were due to leave. Paula and Victoria stayed at the Rookery to man the radio and had a slight panic. Pen sent in a message via the ARGOS from his expedition which they both misread as: "Help - 4 polar bears!" It took a couple of minutes to realise that it was in fact: "No. 4.- We are all OK!" (They had a different code to us) (see Appendix 2).

Just as they were recovering from their shock and as Bravo were getting on the plane, Alpha sent an ARGOS saying not to come as the weather had closed in. What were they to do? They radioed First Air: at first no answer, but eventually they got through. Bravo then had to get off the plane again - in tears - the pressure of it all made everyone very tense. Eventually the pilots decided to hope for the best and took off for the ice. However they had to spend the night in Eureka as the weather had worsened again, but the next morning the changeover was effected.

We met Duncan, a member of Pen's Magnetic North Pole trip. He had had to come off the ice because of quite severe frostbite. Apparently it was not life threatening, but serious enough. Poor man, how frustrating, but a lesson to us all how easy it was to get it.

Later on we moved house, down to No. 75. It was chaos. We had to move the bunk beds, which had been 'borrowed' from Crystal City. They had been nailed to the wall at Gary and Diane's, so when they were moved, they fell to bits. We reassembled them so that the bottom person slept on the floor, it all looked very unsafe. Victoria and I shared the double bed. She was extremely pernickety and could be maddening. Luckily we didn't keep each other awake! It was quite a squash in the house, with five of us.

Victoria:

Mum snored all night and always nicked the blankets. How Dad has survived thirty odd years of marriage to her I will never know!

Sue:

Geoff talked to us in the morning about navigation by the sun, and the movements of the Magnetic North Pole. It moves elliptically fifteen kilometres north each year, and a point is decided annually to be the Magnetic North Pole, the actual position depending on sunspots. Another problem that arises in the Arctic with navigation is that you can set up camp for the night, with your footprints coming from the south, however, during the night the current turns you round and the footprints

86

come from the north! Unless you check your position you could end up going the wrong way!

We began to realise how serious our training was as Geoff began on the do's and don'ts of the Arctic. If you fall in, do not necessarily put up the tent and change, just keep walking and get warm! We got back to the house and more informative talks from Geoff followed. He always used old cardboard boxes for anything he wrote. Very economical, but when you spend thirty months in the Antarctic you learn to save everything. He kept coming out with little sayings, such as - FEAR - Fuck Everything and Run, or Face Everything and Recover! Another gem was - THE SEVEN P'S - Prior Planning and Preparation Prevents a Piss Poor Performance! He told us the story of a pair of travellers in the Arctic who had had a supper of sardines, went to bed, and one of them was woken up by some very strong fishy breath. He complained to his companion and told him to turn over, only to discover that it was an inquisitive polar bear. Luckily they managed to frighten it off, but ate no more sardines.

We went up Beacon Hill, behind the village, by now needing a spot of fresh air. It was quite a blow, and a marvellous view looking down to Resolute, so called because the ship Resolute was here and the village was named after it. Fast ice is joined on to land, and was what we trained on. Pack ice was the ice on which we would be walking. Over the next few days we were to learn how the Arctic works and all the various terminology required when talking about the Arctic.

The ice is held together by pressure, but the moment this is released, (usually due to the movement of the ice caused by the current of the sea), the ice splits and can open up extremely quickly to form large expanses of open water sometimes with 'banks' as much as a mile apart. This open water is referred to as a lead. When the pressure is exerted again, the ice is pushed back together. If there was no current the ice would join up very neatly, but this is the sea, consequently when the ice banks are pushed towards each other they crash together like tectonic plates and form ridges, sometimes only a couple of feet high (rubble), but frequently ten foot plus (pressure ridges). This constant movement is what gives the Arctic its magical feel as the landscape changes minute by minute.

We went up to Gary and Diane's for our Easter Dinner: ham and buffalo steaks, delicious after the rations. The other big treat was fresh vegetables, they are really unknown, or incredibly expensive. Penguin Alpha were there, on a complete high, they had got back that afternoon, having had a successful changeover with Bravo. They had finally crossed the 84th parallel, which was excellent news. They gave us tips and told how they all fell into leads (separately), but only up to their knees, unlike what the press reported.

There had been major problems with the press back in the UK. The story said that Ann Daniels had fallen in and nearly died, but in actual fact she had only gone in up to her knees. A radio programme then followed the story up and had the audacity to ring up Ann's mother to ask her how she felt. It was the first that she knew of it because Ann, (quite rightly) had not felt it was very serious and so was going to tell her when she got home. Not surprisingly Ann's mother was very tearful when told all this - live on air. Later Ann was played this while she was on air. Luckily she had her wits about her and told them exactly what she thought about the whole thing. Another story went around that Sue

Fullilove had been attacked by a polar bear!

There followed a quick lesson on the intricacies of going to the loo in sub zero temperatures. Since paper is precious and adds to the weight of the sledge, you use snow wedges, or wet wipes for your face - the latter are then re-used as loo paper. Apparently they did actually reprocess *The Horse Whisperer*, after everyone had read each page it was used as loo paper!

We heard all about life in the tent, listening to them made it sound a lot less frightening, which was a great help mentally. They told us about their meeting with Polar Free, who later commented on their cheerfulness, their lack of sunburn and general well-being. The best piece of advice they gave us was not to wear bras as they absorb too much sweat.

Caroline Hamilton had flown in from London, just for a three day visit. It must have been very exciting seeing her brainchild come to fruition, but like the rest of us she did seem a little lost on first arrival.

The next day Alpha flew home. It was strange saying good-bye to them; their whole Arctic experience had ended and ours was just about to begin.

Chapter Five

The Ice Mice

Sue:

The final stage of training began. We had to sort out the kit that came back with Penguin Alpha - in order to save costs the different teams were sharing sledges, sleeping bags, parkas and the fur trims round our sledging suits. Once we had these bits of fur on we did feel much more like intrepid Arctic explorers. We had to practise lighting stoves and lanterns, which of course in the end we did not need as it was daylight the whole time. Most exciting of all was fitting our skis. Once on the ice we found skiing with the skins on our skis very different from downhill skiing. Geoff set off quickly, we followed him but soon realised that though we all skied at different paces, it was important to keep together as a team, so we had to adjust our speed.

Victoria:

Skiing was much easier than I had thought, although it was very strange not going downhill. We went round a most amazing iceberg, - a beautiful blue, just like a Fox's Glacier Mint. In the evening we did a lot of adjusting to our suits, which was soon to become a daily routine e.g. mending zips or putting pockets into them. It was a great feeling finally to be doing what we had come here for. I cooked supper with the rations, the last spoonful was a bit much as we had put the butter ration in it. Once on the ice each of us would be eating nearly half a pound of butter every day!

Sue:

It was time to measure up the harnesses and head off onto the ice with our sledges, which are called pulks. It was not as bad as we had anticipated but we were not very good. We went up and over some small pressure ridges and across a few chasms. We were later to learn that the one foot gaps we were crossing were in fact nothing and soon became second nature once out on the ice.

We saw the giant icebergs, they were a blue, blue colour and had been pushed up in circles, which then split in the middle forming passages of pale icy aquamarine. Fresh seawater had appeared round the edge, a slushy pale blue. All the crevasses - the cracks that appeared in the ice - were because of the tide coming in and out every day. When standing still you could hear the cracking underneath. Victoria managed to fall head first into a hole, a very funny sight, with her skis waving in the air.

We found it quite a struggle learning how a pulk moves. For example, you are pulling very hard because it will not budge and then suddenly the ice that has been stopping it gives, and the pulk shoots forward. If you are not quick enough it will hit you, so anticipation is needed to judge when it will move. At that moment you move forward yourself so as to keep the momentum going.

We also learned how to cross obstacles. There is no point just going over yourself and hoping the sledge will follow, too often it won't. What you do is you get to the obstacle yourself, pull your sledge right up beside or behind you, cross the obstacle, and then pull your sledge across with the rope that joins it to your harness. It sounds easy, but can be very tricky if you fall over the far side of a ridge, because gravity is pulling the sledge down the near side and you are being pulled backwards. It requires either amazing dexterity or team work. When pulling pulks a big stride makes an enormous difference - we both found it relatively easy as we take long steps and were also a lot heavier than the others and therefore needed less 'pull' to make the pulk move.

We came across a frozen polar bear foot print, Geoff reckoned that it was at least two months old. Scary but at least it was old! We also had some husky puppies playing around us that day, but they were not used to love and affection from humans so were very nervous at first.

Victoria:

We felt like real polar explorers now we had the skis and the pulks. Having mastered the art of pulking our main worry now was discomfort, i.e. damp clothes in the morning and damp bedding .This was a difficult time for Sue Self as she always got the last choice of equipment - the fifth pair of skis, the fifth pulk etc. She was very good about it though. It really looked like a Chinese laundry in our rooms as there were bits of string everywhere with clothes draped all over them trying to dry: gloves, hats, socks.

On our arrival at Resolute we all had this illusion that polar adventure was some sort of idealistic world and that all explorers were honest and trustworthy. Unfortunately these illusions were shattered fairly rapidly by the First Air pilots, who fly everyone on and off the ice. They told us many stories, such as when the aeroplanes pick the explorers up off the ice and then put them down further on towards the Pole. Eventually it gets out, but only locally. However the First Air pilot, Greg, said that there was only one way to describe our expedition, which was 'honest', the nicest compliment anyone could have given us.

Sue:

It is hard to describe the amazing wasteland that was Resolute, a wilderness of ice and ridges leading up to the hills on either side of the bay. You could see where the stream beds came down in the folds of the hills, but there was never much water in the summer. The drinking water for the village came from a lake up in the hills, and as the top is frozen all winter, the pipes that fed it were kept way down in the bottom of the lake. Every week the water lorry went to the houses in the top village and filled up the tanks. In the bottom village, the Inuit one, the flow of the water prevented it freezing, a ring circuit of water.

The whole landscape here is such a scene of desolation, survival is a long running battle, but despite this, there is a very harsh beauty. We were so lucky to be there. Our main thoughts were that if the last team got to the North Pole we would have achieved a world first, in a slightly unorthodox way. It was fingers crossed all round. We began to realise how privileged we were to be able to experience life in the High Arctic.

It was hard to accept that, though we were so far away from home and in such a different environment, we did not really miss it as much as expected. It was a different world. We did a lot of thinking and realised that you have got to do what you want in life, it's too short to waste time thinking about what you would like to do, so go out and do it. For me, having no dependent children and an understanding husband meant that suddenly I realised what opportunities there are for the taking and how much there is to see and experience. I felt that the real problem would be when I got back home and had to decide where to go next!

Victoria:

I thought a lot about my job and realised that I did not enjoy London any more. Recruitment was great, but I was just not cut-throat enough for the business world.

Little things certainly pleased you up here, going to the Co-op is as exciting as shopping in Harrods. We bought some eggs and bacon, needless to say very expensive and probably well past the sell by date, and cooked the most wonderful supper.

We started to set ourselves targets, but Nobby, Mike and Pen were telling us just to go as far as we could and not worry about goals, though we wanted to reach the 87th parallel, a distance of 110 miles. Apparently if Scott's expedition to the South Pole had just covered another hundred yards a day, they would have got there first. So many if onlys. Penguin Alpha had had the physical time, it was up to us to pick up the speed and put the miles in.

Sue:

April 1st saw our first night on the ice. Now we were indeed Ice Mice. We spent the morning practising erecting the tent, and started walking in the afternoon; pulling our pulks for the first time with a real load in them, about 100lbs. Eventually we reached the two giant ice-bergs and put up the tent. It was octagonal, almost like a circus tent, supported by a ski in the middle, more skis on the guy ropes, which then had the tension tightened by putting the ski poles up against the edge of the tent. There was no ground sheet, just a snow floor, as it would be quite a weight to carry.

When up, two go inside to light up the stoves and get a bowl of soup ready, two shovel snow on to the valances, which helps keep the wind out and anchors the tent, and the other pair set up the radio. There are washing lines in the top of the tent, with safety pins, so that when you hang your damp clothes there each evening the hot air rises and dries your kit, but it was vital to remove everything before bedtime or else they froze. The tent could be put up very quickly and while this was happening, Geoff put out the polar bear wire at a height of about three foot, fixed to an alarm. The outdoor people also cut snow blocks chopped into one foot chunks to melt for water.

Last thing at night we filled the water bottles and then slept with them in our bags. This was to ensure that we had some melted water to help start boiling up in the morning, and bed was the only place where it would not freeze! It was very important to have a fairly high liquid intake, approximately four litres per day, as dehydration could become a problem. From making camp to actually going to bed was almost three hours. It seemed to take for ever.

Victoria:

Everything in the tent lived in your side pockets or else in stuff sacks, and it was vital to be very organised as it was a really tight squeeze in the tent with all six of us. Mum, however, was not a natural camper and she frequently lost her tea bags!

Getting into the sleeping bag at night was pure bliss, it could have been a hard floor or a feather mattress, it did not matter, we just slept. Admittedly you did have to share your sleeping bag with all your damp clothes to help dry them out, not ideal sleeping conditions.

Sue:

When we lay in bed we could hear the ice cracking as the tides washed in and out of the bay. It was a strange feeling during our first night on the ice. You felt in a sort of No Man's Land, it was not land, but it did not feel like the sea. When lying in your bag it was vital not to breathe into it, as your breath froze. Your body actually loses nearly a litre of water during the night. The ice melts in the morning, which causes the bags to be damp, and once outside the tent this moisture freezes and adds extra weight to an already heavy sledge. I kept my gloves on overnight, which did help with the warmth, but the luxury of the hot water bottles was the best part of sleeping. At night you had to pull the draw string tight round the top of the boots so they were not too frozen to put on in the morning, but it was quite a hard struggle to get into them as they had became rigid over night.

We would wake up at about six and our suits were rigid, you had to ease them free. Trying to slide into damp, but stiff red suits was not an enjoyable experience first thing in the morning, but you did get dressed very quickly. The moment everyone had their clothes on it was necessary to knock the roof of the tent, and brush the sides to get rid of the ice crystals before starting the stoves, otherwise they turned to water. Our suits dried a little when cooking, and once we had poured all our hot water into the saucepan and had a hot drink we all felt much better and warmed up. My absolute luxury was my Lapsang tea bag.

Victoria:

I slept very well considering I was in a big black condom, but I found it really very claustrophobic. I was far too hot and Mum was fairly

97

cold, so we each needed to work out our own individual method of sleeping. By the end I slept in only my thermals, and kept my head out at night with just a balaclava covering it. Mum went to the other extreme and wore pretty much everything. Consequently she could hardly move and had to be zipped into her bag each night by me!

Sue:

To pack away the tent you had first to empty all the pockets, or else things got lost or damaged, then put all the gear in the middle and collapse it. Having just come out of a 'warm' tent the temperature outside feels excruciatingly cold, so it was vital to wear your down jacket, even if it made it virtually impossible to move around. It only took us about five minutes to warm up once we had got going, not nearly as bad as we had expected, and in some ways it was warmer than the Brecon Beacons training weekend. It was so cold that within five minutes of walking your eyelashes had frozen up, and the fur on the hoods became white with frozen breath. To begin with we did worry that our eyelashes might snap off in the cold, luckily it was just our imaginations running wild!

Victoria:

That first morning I asked myself if I would go back again. At that moment I thought I probably would, because you put up with the discomforts for the pure beauty and joy of such a place. I thought I might well say something different in a few weeks time.

Back in the UK I had seen an article on the Internet which posed a similar question: 'Why do so many explorers risk their lives to travel north on skis, often solo and without resupply. For many reasons humans like challenges, and the polar expedition is the ultimate challenge, says Richard Weber. In 1995 Weber and Micha Malakov achieved the first unsupported trek to the North Pole and back. People chose the Pole   because of its unique location. It is a route pioneered in the last century, so there is a historical reason to take that particular path.

Sue:

After lunch we went back to the Rookery to pack the rest of our provisions, helped by Duncan, who (we later discovered when on the ice) had cut some dreadful jokes from a Viz magazine and put them in with the food! We had various faxes waiting for us from friends and families. It is amazing what a morale booster it is to know that everyone is thinking of us. We sent off our messages, which did help us feel in touch with the real world, but time seemed to mean much less here, perhaps because of all the hours of sunlight. Outside there was a mirage, which we saw several days running. Somerset Island was reflected into the sky across the bay, you could see great white icebergs in front of it; this was quite a usual occurrence. The other effect you can have is ice blink, a luminous reflection off the ice. The sun sometimes had strange rings round it, or an extra sun - the dog sun.

Next morning we packed twenty two fuel containers. It was vital to protect them, as leaked fuel meant not only running out of fuel but also damaged equipment. In the worst case scenario it could also lead to contaminated food, though usually the food and fuel were kept separately.

Later on that day we visited Terry's (The High Arctic Hotel). After entering through the back door you arrived at the kitchen where everyone ate. Past this were rambling sitting down areas with dormitory style bedrooms leading off. All very simple, but warm and friendly. While there we met a British couple who were planning to take a group of eleven to fifteen year olds to Resolute the following year. The amount of planning and preparation that they were having to put into their expedition was staggering. Not only did they have to try and raise large amounts of money, but the potential risks involved in taking children to such a hostile environment were massive. As we left Terry's I think that we all had visions of the old fashioned school trip to a local museum being replaced by trips to the North and South Poles!

We also met up with Pen's group of solicitors (sponsored by Oyez) who had skidooed to the Magnetic North Pole. They said that it was intensely cold. They had pulks like ours, pulled them for ten minutes on the first day, and decided that it was no way to spend a holiday so tied them to the skidoos and pulled them that way. By the end they only had one skidoo working, having written off two others! They had obviously had a marvellous time, having nearly set the tent on fire, almost shot themselves, and sung hymns from A&M each night after reading Winnie the Pooh to each other! In the end they had been lifted off from where they were and were dropped at the Magnetic North Pole. Unfortunately, Pen was in trouble with the police because he should have had a permit when he was taking his party on their expedition, as one has to have permission to go through Polar Bear Pass. It was rather a hairy sounding place!

Victoria:

We all were beginning to realise the total size and wilderness of

100

the North West Territories, it covers nearly a third of Canada. Europe is very cosy but this was a real wilderness and we felt very much on the edge of it. We were way past the tree line - not a single tree grows in this region as the average July temperature is below 10°C. There was nothing beyond apart from ice, islands and mountains, and of course, always the ocean, and beyond that our goal, the North Pole.

Sue:

What we liked about Resolute was that everyone knew exactly what was happening expedition-wise. It was a very small place, a bit like Mull. Our main worry now was the unexpected. We were being gently introduced to the whole scene, and it made us realise how much there was to learn about everything. For Sue Self, it must have been very frustrating, knowing she would not be going out. She had quite a tough inner core, but we felt that her being there made it much harder for us to become a team, as there was always a slight restraint. You felt you could not mention the expedition too much, or how you felt about it, and it was hard to talk about nervousness, you felt she was almost waiting for one of us to drop out through illness or otherwise. We were probably having more of a problem developing the team spirit. However, having said that, we did feel that we developed into a cohesive group, and got to know each other really well. Victoria seemed to talk nonstop, I never realised just what a chatterbox she was - though it got better when everyone told her to shut up!

Our four day training trip started on Saturday 5th April. We were up at 7.00 am and ready for the off having loaded our pulks and headed down to the shore. In another place, a little warmer perhaps,

101

No. 75 would have been an ideal holiday cottage, one minute from the beach.

During the first part of the trip we were pulling about 110 lbs. We went straight out into the bay and into the rubble, ice chunks in no particular order, just like a packet of Fox's Glacier Mints dumped on the ice and scattered all over the place, through which you have to pull your pulk. This insists on getting jammed between the chunks, and you then have to turn round and either heave it out of a hole or pull it round the ice. In a way it was much more fun than the flat pans (where you went a good deal faster) because it was a challenge, a bit like a jigsaw puzzle when you have to pick the best route. Somehow the scenery and the satisfaction of doing the difficult bits made it all worth while. We soon realised that the verb 'to man haul' was a very strenuous one.

The rubble soon levelled off into a flat pan or two, followed by some icebergs where we practised climbing for a while. By now the wind had got up and we walked to the west of Resolute, eventually stopping by a huge glacier. The day was divided up into hour long marches, and we did six. The hard part was the monotony; an hour seems to take forever, and we were always convinced that the timekeeper had miscalculated.

By 4 pm it was time to stop, but it was very difficult to put the tent up, as the wind was blowing at 15 knots and felt very icy. We tried to imagine if any of our friends would be crazy enough to do this, but pretty much drew a blank. One rarely walks more than six miles in a day, but you had to keep going; there was no way out, and it did get depressing sometimes.

The tent almost took off during the night, and the next morning it was still blowing a gale. We all had to wrap up warm in all the clothes we had in order to get the tent down very quickly. With the wind chill it was at least -50⁰C. We were, without doubt, four very frigid women!

Victoria:

While you are walking you think about everything from life, work, men, the M6, to breakfast at Le Duc. It is a strange feeling, as your thoughts do not last for very long. You also wonder what the hell you are doing here. I thought of Annabelle Spink at 10.30 am (5.30 pm UK time): she would be at her wedding reception - what a contrast! I felt exhausted and my back hurt, but it cheered me up to think my bottom and thighs must be shrinking! I cooked supper that night, Big Ben's Bean Feast, probably the most disgusting meal I have ever eaten, I had two thirds of it and gave up. Never again.

Sue:

We set off that morning walking directly into the wind. It was bitter, but gradually eased off. It was one of those days when you wonder why on earth you are doing this trip. The morning was very, very windy, bitterly cold and there was rubble for most of the time. The afternoon warmed up, but by that stage we were all very sweaty as we had left our wind-proof jackets on. So we got even colder when we stopped, as all the sweat froze. We should have removed them when we were warm.

The wind blowing the snow created the most magical effects which did not seem to help me, I found it very hard work. But everyone has to have a bad day at some stage. That evening remained bad. It was my turn to cook dinner, I felt absolutely freezing cold and never seemed to get warm. We had a fairly hellish day. I was very worried at one stage that I had frost bite in my hand, but it was just that the tireder you are the colder you feel. But that is what the training was about, learning how to survive comfortably. Having survived the miseries of that day, we all felt that we could do it.

Victoria:

Paula really annoyed me as she had a go at me for something I never even did. Tempers were definitely frayed. Mum walked too fast and did not wait for anyone else, and Sue Self's pulk kept on falling over, it drove us all bonkers. Luckily we were honest enough to tell each other what we thought so there were no hard feelings.

Sue:

Before we set out we had wondered what on earth we would do for the rest of the day if we only had six hours sledging, but once we had stopped it took three hours to sort ourselves out. We were all given numbers, I was No. 1, Lynne No. 2, Paula No. 3 and Victoria No. 4. Each had a different job, Lynne and I did the water, Paula did the radio and Victoria was inside the tent, doing the jobs there, a cushy number! Lynne and I also had to shovel the snow onto the valances. My place in the tent was a busy one as I had to pass in all the ice chunks which were required for melting into water.

We all felt at times that Geoff was over fussy and too particular, but he was training us and teaching us a routine, and the order of things helped us to run our lives more efficiently once on the ice. It was the same sort of routine both night and morning: at least three hours of

104

getting water boiling, filling water bottles, having at least two hot drinks each, and either eating breakfast or supper.

Sleeping was the worst part of the training. Having done up all your zips, right round your head, pulling the condom completely over you, you were nice and warm to begin with, but by half way through the night your breath would have crystallised and started to fall onto your face. It was probably warmer to lie on your back, but more comfortable on your side. I did have a problem keeping warm, my feet were always toasty, but not my top. I was worried about frostbite when I woke up in the middle of the night and realised that my hand was completely numb. In a terrible panic, I shook it hard, full of the thought that for me the expedition would be over, and there would be five fingers missing, but then the feeling came back and I realised that rather than having severe frostbite, I had been lying on it and it had gone to sleep!

We heard Penguin Bravo on the radio doing their evening transmission. They had done nine miles which was very good going, they hoped to get to the 85th parallel the next day. By now the relay had done one hundred miles, only three hundred and seventeen to go.

Victoria:

Geoff taught us very early on that it was not in fact necessary to have frozen suits each morning. The reason was very simple: we had all been wearing too many clothes, and as we pulled our sledges along we sweated, and this sweat quickly froze as soon as we stopped walking. If we could learn to wear fewer clothes, and perhaps be slightly colder when stopping for a break, we would sweat less and therefore not have rigid suits each morning.

Sue:

Sue Self told us a joke -

Baby : Mum, am I a polar bear?

Mum : Yes. I am and Dad is, so you must be.

Baby : Dad, am I a polar bear?

Dad : Yes. I am and Mum is, so you must be. Why do you ask?

Baby : Because I'm f...ing freezing!!

The next day we came across polar bear droppings. They were obviously scavengers, real rubbish tip stuff, bits of plastic, seal meat and undigested bones. There were more polar bear footprints, a mother and her cub. (Useful tip - if you do have to shoot a polar bear, do not eat its liver as it is deadly poisonous apparently!) A favourite Geoff saying: 'What I hear I forget, what I see I remember, what I do I know.' We had a really good day, achieving five or six miles, mainly over rubble and very flat ice to finish with.

Victoria:

I was beginning to smell and was convinced that I had mis-aimed when going to the loo. Upon investigation I decided that everything was vaguely all right! But even after wet wipes I still stank, it was quite disgusting. Paula later admitted that she was also suffering! We had all learnt an important lesson: a strip wash on a regular basis is essential. It does not matter how basic it is but it is vital, if only for the sake of your tent companions.

We were now looking at a changeover with Penguin Bravo on the Thursday, or possibly Friday. I felt I would rather have Friday! I was knackered, and was terrified about going on the ice, but after two years of waiting and training it was great to be finally ready, and to know that at last every step would be in the right direction!

The most frustrating thing about the dress rehearsal was that it did not count, since we were walking in circles. I had been advised by an Antarctic expert I had met to chop up old karrimats and put them under your feet while sitting in the tent, as every layer of insulation counts. I also had some big hiccups with the zip round my crotch: every time I undid it, it got stuck. Poor Mum had to sort it out, something only a mother could do!

When we were walking in single file Geoff always ended up walking with Mum, they seemed to talk endlessly!

Sue:

We spent our last night on the actual shore, and next morning we walked up a beautiful stream, frozen of course, that ended up in a really steep gully, a big struggle pulling the pulks up, and, as usual, there was Nobby, filming us. We then went up a shorter, and even steeper one and we all had to loose off our sledges as it took all five of us to pull each sledge up, quite hard work.

We began to realise what Scott meant when he said: "No journey made with dogs can approach that fine conception which is realised when a party of men is forced to meet the hardships, dangers and difficulties with their own unaided efforts, and by days and weeks of hard physical labour succeed in solving some problem of the great unknown."

It was lovely just chilling out. We showered and, heavens, our underwear was disgusting. They needed two goes with the washing machine! We would definitely be wearing our Arctic knickers. My own design, size eighteen knickers, unpicked along the gusset, velcro sewn on each side, and worn with pantie liners, just like having a clean pair every day! Poor Nobby was explaining how Matty had radioed in to ask for Tampax. He went to the shop, saw three sizes, so described her (Matty) to the shopkeeper to get the right size! The base camp team must have learned a lot about women! Nobby also plucked up courage to say that all Penguin Alpha 'trimmed' themselves to help with smells. We were not sure whether we wanted to go that far.

We all felt quite tired after the dress rehearsal and were slightly dreading going on the ice. Consequently we now did not mind that our changeover was definitely going to be Friday instead of Thursday. We all knew that the next time we pulled our pulks it would be the real thing; we were very excited but also terrified. At least we would be walking north by then, it all seemed such a waste, our walks round Resolute.

Victoria:

There were more faxes for us all, which was very comforting and they really did lessen the feeling of isolation. I had excellent news from the UK that two of my friends, John and Sam, had got engaged. News travels fast even to the Arctic! The other news we heard was that the IRA had been putting bombs on the motorway and apparently stopped the Grand National. It all seemed so far away though, we could not really comprehend it.

Sue:

It was now just a matter of finally getting sorted before we went off, and everyone wanted to get on with it. The problem with the changeovers is that you cannot afford to make mistakes: the flights were the most expensive part of the whole expedition. To drop us was going to cost £7,000, Delta would be £9,000, £18,000 to drop Echo and £25,000 to pick them up, as by then two aeroplanes would be needed. In theory each team would be walking further than the one before, as the going got better the nearer you were to the Pole. In the end of course, it would depend on conditions.

The final briefings took place and Pen made a very valid comment: 'There are only two speeds at the Pole, stationary and slow. The only way to do Polar travel is steadily and surely. It is not a race.' Pen felt that women have been brainwashed into thinking they cannot do Arctic travel. They might not have the brawn, but they approach problems in a different, less macho, way, and use their brains differently. In fact, they have every chance of success. Particularly us, because we came to it with no pre-conceived ideas.

By now Sue Self had been whisked away - it had been realised that it was difficult for both her and us; she because she knew in no way would she be able to go onto the ice, and for us because we did have some feeling of, not guilt exactly, but pity for her. It must have been dreadful seeing everyone going out nervous and coming back on a high.

It was then back to No. 75 to finish our personal packing having left our sledges at First Air. (See Appendix 5.) We were all quite quiet and nervous at this stage. Suddenly Geoff appeared, with various sheets of paper which contained his favourite poems. He then proceeded to read us some: 'The Killing of Dan McGrew' amoungst others. We spent some time talking as a group, trying to psych ourselves up. We worked well as

109

a team, we were all very different and at times wound each other up, but ultimately it was very important to be honest with each other and to learn to work together.

It was the sort of waiting during the lull before the storm, and even Victoria was being quiet. I did think of Jeremy and what he must be going through. He is a worrier anyway, and his imagination was probably running wild. I hoped that he would be reassured by the training we had been put through. I was lucky in that I felt totally confident that we would be all right. It was all part of the 'thinking positive' that has always been part of my attitude to life.

Friday 11th April. It was either a wonderful or a ghastly day, we were not sure which! This was the day we were meant to be leaving for the ice. We got up feeling very jittery knowing that we were on standby. Originally we should have left the day before, but Matty had said that Penguin Bravo were having problems with their ski bindings, so some were flown in from Iqualit on the Thursday flight. They then had to be fitted, which took a fair amount of time, but were ready for our departure on Friday. We could not see what was wrong with the old ones, and thought that we could have easily flown in on Thursday, when the weather would not have been the problem it proved to be next day.

Victoria:

Psychologically it was very difficult to have to change all our bindings, because our skis were also changed; we had all become attached to our own skis. I had put smiley faces on mine as well as Tessa's paw prints! It sounds silly, but emotions were running high at the time and it was the last thing we needed. The final straw was that we would

110

not even have tried the bindings properly before we got onto the ice.

Sue:

At 8.30 am we were told that changeover probably could not happen because of a deterioration in the weather. It was extremely irritating because the pilots reckoned it would not improve until Saturday or Sunday, in which case we would be very unlikely to get to the 87th parallel. This was always a problem at change-over time The Met. Office said one thing, down on the ice the guides said another, and the satellites seemed to say something completely different. So one had to go along with what the pilots said, as they did have years of experience.

We had a day messing about, playing cards, trying our skis very briefly, with their new bindings - anything to try and not think about the wait, and what we could well be doing in forty eight hours time. We started playing some Irish music and Victoria and I demonstrated reeling. Eventually we were all doing it, when in walked Mike who said that the one thing he could not stand was bossy women doing reels! We had a chance for a bit more bonding, as Sue Self had spent the day before with Geoff fixing on the new bindings, and had then stayed up at the Rookery. We were all a lot more open with each other, and had long discussions about the politics and controversy of the selection process.

Victoria:

I found it very hard that Mum, who was twenty odd years older than me, was probably stronger both mentally and physically. It was very difficult to accept that and at times I almost had a feeling that

111

perhaps I would not have been there if Mum had not been selected. Was I just part of the PR duo. It was difficult for me, especially on a bad day.

*

Internet report

When Penguin Bravo started their leg on Sunday 30 March the scheduled changeover day was Thursday 10 April. Problems with ski bindings reported back from the ice last Monday evening have caused everyone a few headaches in finding a solution. It also led to a decision being made to push the changeover day to Friday.

On Tuesday when this decision was made the forecast was for the weather to become more rather than less stable as the week progressed. A reasonable basis for the decision? No such luck. Thursday dawns in Resolute; sunny, clear and windless. Let's hope it is the same tomorrow - is the thought on the mind of Penguin Bravo on the ice and Penguin Charlie back in Resolute - hanging around is not good for the nerves or for the expedition's progress.

Mid afternoon, the jet arrives from down South with the spare binding parts the ice team need. Eight hours later, the work on the ski bindings are complete after some fairly major hacksaw surgery conducted by Sue Self, the MPPR's official reserve. Alas, the Arctic weather report showing up on the satellite maps is now not so favourable. Charlie retire to bed hopeful, but doubtful that they will be on the Twin Otter the next morning, to start what they have been building up to for twenty months or so.

The 07.00 radio call from Bravo informs us that the weather is good for changeover. The weather forecast suggests the opposite. One hour later Bravo inform us that things are not looking so bright. The

08.30 satellite pass photo gives more bad news. To add salt to the wound, the outlook for Saturday is even more grim. Charlie are stood down and proceed to keep themselves distracted from the building tension by starting a mid morning session of what the less informed among us are told is reeling. Bravo are left to their own devices. **End**.

*

Sue:

We decided to have a treat that evening, to cheer ourselves up. We had found some steaks in the freezer, so got them out to defrost and I was going to cook some gastronomic delight. However, at 5.50 pm, the door burst open, Mike walked in and told us that we had to be at the airport by 6.30 pm, so this was it. We had packed and repacked our stuff sacks about four times that day, but Geoff was very insistent that we should check one more time, but it was a rush. We also had to leave all the rest of our gear neatly, as Delta would be moving in that evening. We had to boil up water for our bottles, make a few sandwiches for supper. Geoff drove us up to the airfield, where we hung around for what seemed like hours.

We got quite cold, there was a bitter wind blowing, the snow was swirling around and the inactivity mixed with worry and impatience made us very tense. Paula had to have a cigarette, Geoff told her to get well away from the planes when smoking, and we then saw a mechanic repairing an aircraft with a cigarette dangling out of his mouth.

The weather appeared to be closing in and we felt that if we did not depart now it would be too late, another day would be lost. We waited in the hangar as it was getting colder. One of the mechanics had just

113

made a wonderful pizza, and offered us all a slice, the best one ever! At last the time came to load our pulks onto the plane, plus what seemed like huge amounts of bits. Nobby was to come with us, plus of course his video camera. We had to say goodbye to Sue Self, which was difficult for everyone. So, just before 8 pm, we climbed into the Twin Otter and took off.

Victoria:

I was so scared I did not want to go. I felt utterly petrified and alone. I knew we would be back in only a couple of weeks time but was so scared I was a bit tearful, Nobby gave me a big hug on the runway to cheer me up, and then proceeded to interview me!

Sue:

In the air it was amazing going over the land which you have been living on, but haven't really had the chance to get to know or explore properly. It was flattish but you could see the contours, such as winding rivers, hills, rocks, but so barren. Then, as we came to the edge of Cornwallis Island, there were the rivers running down to the sea, the shore line was very clear and the ripple effect of the sea freezing against the land. It was like being above the clouds, but actually you are not. It was land, but because it is all white, height becomes impossible to gauge.

We had become accustomed to having no colour, and seeing the evening sun reflecting on patches of ice was a wonderful sight; there was a double sun reflected in the sky. Time seemed to lose its meaning when the sun was up all day and most of the night. We were aiming to land at three or four in the morning but by that time we were going to be so far

114

north that there would be no night, and it would be no problem landing. We wondered if people had ever lived here, or had it always been frozen, or did they come here in the summer rather as in Norway? With green, rolling hills it would be like the lowlands of Scotland.

After about four hours we arrived at Eureka - a weather station on Ellesmere island, the most northerly post office in the world. Only the Air Force station at Alert, to the north east, is nearer the Pole. We radioed in to the weather station, and asked them to pick us up and take us down to the base while the plane was refuelling. It was surreal. We raced down the runway towards the rubbish tip to look for wolves. They were not there, but an Arctic hare was. So back to the station. It was 11.15 pm.

Twelve people live on the base operating the weather station and the air strip. The summer months there are the busiest, as the military use the island for exercises, and have a base there. We were a rarity: women! The men were very pleased to see us! The sun was out, the moon was out - it was midnight. We left Eureka at 12.15 am Ellesmere island was stunning, a geography lesson from the air: oxbows, glaciers, fjords, the highest peak there is 2,216 metres. Everyone had a go at flying the plane, it was exciting to be flying due north at 2.00 am into the sun. There was no pressure in the plane so you could open the window to take photographs. It was very cramped inside with the sledges. No in flight service. As we left the island, with its vast mountain ranges covered in snow and glaciers we had our first glimpse of the Arctic Ocean as it came against the land. The frozen sea rippled as it touched the shoreline. We were at last on our way.

Part Two

Penguin Charlie

Chapter Six

DIARIES: Stepping Out

Saturday 12ᵗʰ April 1997

Sue:

Soon we left the northern shores and hit some clouds, then came out and saw the pressure ridges. It had been hard to visualise them before. Then we saw open leads - terrifying. The pilots are highly skilled and can land in the most inhospitable areas. When we found the landing strip, the weather having become misty meant we had to circle round and round and round, over leads, and large masses of snow and ice, it was quite 'white knuckle'. It was a thrilling moment, seeing Penguin Bravo's blue and yellow tent looming out of the mist, with all the dancing red figures, quite an emotional feeling.

Each time we went past I thought we won't land, we'll go back to Eureka. But land we did, having spent half an hour circling round, eventually coming down on a runway marked by two pulks at each end. It seemed a bumpy landing, but later we realised this was excellent, Arctic landings are not quite like Heathrow. We skidded to a halt in front of Bravo's tent, and here we were on the ice, a strange, slightly unworldly feeling: anticipation, but no real idea of what we were going to be faced with. We rushed around, feeling rather shell shocked, trying to help and sort out the gear we were keeping, a sort of organized chaos. We were also slightly dopey having been travelling for over twelve hours, with no sleep or food, (having missed supper). But suddenly all was sorted; Matty and Denise had changed their clothes in the aeroplane, the toy penguin - mascot and relay baton - had been entrusted to us, and the dreaded moment had come, the loneliest moment you can imagine.

The plane takes off, you see it disappearing into the distance, the engine getting quieter and quieter, and there you are, one hundred and fifty miles from land, twelve hours from help, two and a half miles above the ocean bed, floating on large islands of ice. We could only rely on ourselves, what we have in the sledges and our own mental resources; no living off the land, because this isn't land, its the ocean. Self reliance had suddenly become very important. For the first time in our lives we were truly responsible for ourselves and our team, and without the team there would be no survival. Mental strength is almost more important than physical. During our training we decided that it was probably 60:40, but I'm not sure that it is not more like 70% mental and only 30% physical.

By the time everyone had left, we agreed that at 4.45 am it would be better to pitch camp and have a short sleep before getting going again, as we had not had any sleep for nearly twenty four hours. I think we needed time to realise that we were actually here on the ice. We had been thinking of little else for well over a year, and to be suddenly in the middle of what had been a dream up until now was very hard to accept. I think that for all of us the reality of where we were was one of the most difficult issues to face up to.

We were up at 12.45 pm and off at 3.30 pm. Matty and Denise spent a lot of time going through all their papers. We were warned by the others that they would be bit monosyllabic on changeover day. Home seemed a long way away, and they had to get to know a new team.

We walked six and a half hours on our first day, all navigation being by sun or GPS (a state of the art pinpoint navigation system, as used during the Gulf Conflict) as the magnetic variation was a massive

91^0, so compasses did not work very efficiently. Matty carried a gun on the top of her pulk at all times, in case of polar bears. At night it lived outside - if it was brought in, condensation would have formed, which would then have frozen, causing the gun to jam. Her sledge was right by the door, ready for instant access. Polar bears were not the sort of wild life we wanted to meet!

There were some amazing sights. We went across our first lead, it was like jelly or rubber, a bit nerve wracking; the darker the blue the thinner the ice. Some huge blocks of ice were just thrown up, a strange blue colour shining through like electric light. You could feel the bitter cold coming off and because we were quite tired it seemed to penetrate our bodies. The blue was almost ethereal in colour, and as the sun had disappeared and the sky was slightly misty, the light seemed more intense. The wonderful limitless space gave a feeling that we were in a newly created world, totally unspoilt, and the ocean seemed to go on for ever.

The last hour was very hard. I felt exhausted, partly I think because the time was all wrong. I am certainly a morning person, and to be walking really quite late in the evening was difficult. We did not set up camp till 10.30 pm, then there were three hours during which we cooked and boiled our water. Because the sun is up the whole day and night, time has no real meaning and this helps to make you feel rather disorientated.

*

Victoria:

Before we knew what was happening we were on a tiny plane flying low over the stunning mountain range that makes up Ellesmere Island. We were flying directly into the midnight sun and were heading for a place where very few men and women have ever walked before.

The plane suddenly started to bank and coming through the clouds we could see a vast expanse of whiteness that was to be our home for the next three or four weeks. The approach to the 'runway' started. A runway is half a mile by a quarter of a mile of 'flat' ice. The plane prepared to land, we braced ourselves, but the wheels touched and then we took off again. Our hearts sank, what was wrong? We were now twelve hours from Resolute Bay so surely we would not have to turn back. The pilot told us that he had to check that the ice could hold the weight of the plane so he would touch down a few times before actually landing. Great comfort! Four nervous 'explorers' were now terrified. What on earth were we doing here? Our stomachs were somewhere near our feet.

After an eternity, probably half an hour, the plane finally landed. Considering the plane was landing on hard packed ice and snow the pilot managed an incredibly comfortable landing. We only bumped off our seats a couple of times. An hour later, having unloaded all our gear and had a brief catch up with the previous team, we were ready to set off. The plane doors shut and the engines started. It took off and disappeared into the distance, and we were alone on the top of a giant ice cap in the middle of nowhere; eight hundred miles from Resolute Bay, fifteen hours away from the nearest help. I did not know what to feel. A range of emotions went though my mind: I want to go home. I am so lucky to be here. I am so proud to be British. What am I doing? I cannot give up as all my friends, family and the press will think I am a wimp. Help!! There was no time to think as we had to keep moving, or else frostbite would set in. Ahead of us was three weeks of just heading North...

However it was not 'just heading North'. This place which I

was so lucky to be in was without a doubt the most beautiful place on earth. Imagine a landscape with every shade of blue, white and black. The scenery changes every day, literally, as the ice moves apart and crunches together. The Arctic must be the noisiest place on earth. The ice makes a rumbling noise - like a tube train coming out of a tunnel - as it crashes together and the snow/ice crunching under your feet sounds like the first bite of an apple, or the sound of an aeroplane coming out from the clouds. The ice formations would be a geologist's dream. Every type of stalagmite and stalactite imaginable, and all in this beautiful shade of electric blue. Thousands of massive ice chunks that have just been thrown in the air and left as they landed, all higgledy piggledy but still in some kind of Arctic order. The whole scene is just impossible to describe without doing it an injustice.

It was a very strange experience, meeting our guides, Matty and Denise, for the first time when we landed. We were all nervous and excited, and they were very introspective, having just received letters from home, and knowing that the previous team were on their way home to a hot bath, while they still had another two months to go. It must have been very difficult for them.

We decided to set up the tent immediately, as it was 4.00 am and we had been up for twenty two hours. The next morning we got up and walked for six and a half hours. It was a good first day, great for confidence building. The weather was not brilliant, cloudy and windy, and we were all relieved that we had finally done the resupply, as the forecast was for worse weather still. Meeting my first lead was both exciting and an anticlimax. Having heard all these horror stories I was slightly disappointed by this one foot wide stretch of rubbery ice. Little did I know then that it was not typical, as most leads would require a great deal of effort to negotiate.

*

Internet report

Greetings from Penguin Bravo!

Since we are fresh back from the pack ice (only just), we thought we'd explain what was happening from our end while we were waiting for the changeover.

The finale to the changeover drama...

As explained in the last update, there was considerable doubt as to whether the changeover would go ahead or not, right up until the last minute. We were in constant radio coms with the plane (November Alpha November) as it approached our position on the ice, giving updates on the weather as it steadily worsened. From where we were sitting, in our tent on the pack ice, it seemed totally impossible that the pilot would even consider landing, but he insisted on 'giving it a go', so we just stood by to give him as much help as we possibly could from the ground.

The pilot, Paul, gave us an ETA of 03:17 our time, so we sat listening for the sounds of the approaching twin-engined Otter. Finally - there it was, so we dashed outside leaving one of the team by the radio. By this time the ice fog was so thick that we could only just see the outline of the plane as it passed overhead. The pilot couldn't see us at all, although he knew by the GPS that he was over our position. We radioed to tell him he had just overflown us, so he asked that as he made the next pass we would radio when he was directly overhead. This we did, then began a series of nerve-racking passes as he tried to check out the runway. We could hardly see the pulks marking the ends of the 500m strip, but after 8 or 9 passes he obviously decided that everything was OK and made his final approach. We watched with fingers crossed as he came in low through the fog, then at last! Skis made contact and he had done it - much to our and Penguin Charlie's considerable relief. Through good luck (and of course good judgement!), we had picked a very flat airstrip on multi-year ice, with few bumps and very small sastrugi (wind-blown snow ridges which can be up to three feet high), which had helped considerably, but the pilot did an exceptional job. **End**

*

Sunday 13ᵗʰ April
Sue:

We were up at 9.00 am with another three hours spent melting water and eating breakfast. Eventually we were off, soon after 11.45 am. We walked for about seven and a half hours, and the last hour was very hard work. I felt that this was my worst day so far. To begin with we had marvellous flat pans of ice, the ideal terrain. However, they became incredibly boring and tedious. You felt that you would weep from the sheer boredom (but I could not possibly say this to Victoria, as in our house the word 'bored' does not exist.) I have always said that anyone who claims they are bored must have a very empty mind. So here I was, with a very empty mind! Trying to fill it was quite a problem at times, but luckily the Arctic provides solutions, a lump of ice, a mini ridge, all these things distract you.

At times I thought to myself that this was not the place for a fifty something, I should be at home doing my sewing. But did I really mean that? Absolutely not, despite the bad moments this was the best thing that I had ever done, every fifty something needs to be challenged. Your second half century can be just as much a time of discovery as your first years. Already we had seen sights that would always be there in our minds. We were living in a sort of dreamworld, where all thoughts were intensified. When we walked we were all very aware of how each other felt; at every break we gave a mark out of ten, and if someone did not want to talk, all right, you just put your thumb up.

We set up camp at 7.00 pm. After a long hard day it was an enormous effort obtaining the snow blocks. We had to dig enough for both morning and evening, as no-one would want to go outside once we were settled down. Victoria and Matty sorted our things out in the tent; they seemed to get on well together, getting the stoves lit, arranging our sleeping bags, and, best of all, making the soup, chicken noodle, gorgeous to have when we came in, rather tired. The only problem with the soup was that if you put in your lumps of frozen cheese and butter the soup chilled down very rapidly, so it was a matter of gulping it down as fast as possible.

Matty said that she did not like families being together when doing outward bound activities, she always splits them up, so to be stuck with the two of us must have been difficult, as she really wanted us to be in two separate teams. However, I was much more worried about Paula and Lynne being out-Riches-ed! Though because I was aware of this constraint, perhaps I talked less to Victoria than I would normally have done.

I quickly realised that I liked to have Victoria on the same side of a lead as me, especially when it was rubber ice, the kind that bounces gently as you cross it, with the waves sometimes lapping at the edges. We learned that there are various ways to test the ice for safety; if your pole goes in beyond the basket, it is soft ice, dangerous to cross as it is slushy. However, if your pole only goes down an inch, it is rubber ice which is semi-safe to cross as long as it is one at a time. If you have to slam your ski pole through, and the ice is opaque, it is safe to move over, and the best of all is when there is a snow dusting which normally means that the ice is at least four to six inches thick.

*

Victoria:

We covered another six miles, mainly on a bearing West but ended up in the same easterly position as the previous day, the slip East was becoming a serious problem. The expedition was intending to walk due North following the 75th longitude as far as possible. However one tended to forget that we were on a sea and the currents pull you in a variety of directions. By drifting East the whole time we were in danger of getting caught in the currents that move around Greenland and if that happened there was virtually no chance of us reaching the Pole, as however far West we walked each day the strong Greenland currents would pull us further East. Consequently we rarely walked due North, and almost always followed a bearing West or Northwest, very frustrating as you felt that you were having to walk two sides of a triangle. How quickly could we have got there if we could have just walked due North?

It was a beautiful day, the sun shone all day and there was not a breath of wind. All this despite the weather forecast being for storm conditions. We were beginning to realise how unpredictable the Arctic was. We all got boiling hot and stripped down to either our Helly Hansons (a blue thermal suit), our Damarts, or our suit rolled down and tied round our waist. This was supposed to be the place where your flesh freezes within seconds of exposure! Walked for seven hours over lots of bumps and leads, but no major problems. I was feeling pretty strong and loved being at the back, as it was easier to stop and take pictures.

Took lots of photographs of Lukas the bear during the day. Six months previously I had met his owner, Nick Spencer, who explained that Lukas had travelled all over the world and was hopefully going to be auctioned off at some stage for leukaemia. I offered to take him on the expedition, not only because it was a good cause, but because it meant that I could share my sleeping bag with a man each night albeit a very tiny one! The only male on the expedition, he was very honoured.

I still could not believe that I was really there. It was so much easier than training because every footstep was heading in the right direction, in theory. The rubble was not nearly as bad as I had expected, but the leads were very weird. The ice was all wobbly/spongy and it cracked very easily. Denise managed to get her foot wet but was OK. We heard on the radio that the Dutch were only seventeen miles in front of us. That news was enough to motivate us to walk even faster and further, as rumour had it that they were a very good looking bunch of men! Until you are out on the ice you do not realise what a mainstay the radio is. Even if it is purely for giving your position, hearing another voice is just wonderful, and when you receive a message from home it keeps you going for days after.

*

Monday 14th April

Sue:

We saw foxes footprints one hundred and forty miles from land, which could have been worrying, as polar bears sometimes follow fox trails, but luckily we saw none of the dreaded bear prints! Matty and Denise are very keen dog sledders and cannot think why we do not use dogs instead of ourselves. At times I felt they had quite a valid point, and perhaps we were making rather hard work of our journey. On the other hand it would not be half so satisfying if a dog did it all! One of the advantages of dogs is that when you take the sleds out, all you have to do is to set the dogs on the required bearing, guide them for five minutes and they will stay on the same bearing the rest of the day. This is because they have a sort of inbuilt compass. Both guides are totally fanatical about their dogs and Matty even recycles her dead ones, i.e. fur trim for hats and hoods, so nothing is wasted!

It was a very good day. I felt better, and having started at 10.00am we had more walking in the morning. Everyone worked better earlier. We did seven miles in total. A number of flattish pans and not too many pressure ridges. At one stage we came across a lovely frozen lead (two weeks old), which we positively skimmed along. It was quite gorgeous, bits of ice pushed up in layers, frozen ice crystals almost like coral. However the problem was that your skis did tend to stick to the surface of newish ice because it was just congealed salt water, and at the halts we had to scrape this congealed water off our ski skins.

I left off one layer of clothes and decided not to wear my hat, so that I could lose some heat through the top of my head. Overheating was the problem, not cold, as everyone thought it would be. I had definitely

129

overheated the previous day and everything was sopping wet. I had to hang up my suit on the tent pole to dry and in general the day had not been a good one in keeping an even temperature. Penguin Alpha kept talking about the importance of venting, i.e. opening your zips the whole time. It did work, you had to walk on the cool side of warm. The moment that you saw someone's logo on their back growing ice crystals, i.e. frozen sweat, you told them to stop, and try and cool down by opening a zip or two. A lot of time seemed to be spent in adjusting our clothes.

Victoria had more problems with her crap flap zip. There we were, in the Arctic, a very grown up environment, and a voice shouts 'Mum, come and help me!' I thought I was escaping that! But to be able to share an experience like the Arctic with a family member is wonderful. During the hard parts of the day, which conversely are the easy flat pans, I spent time thinking of Jeremy and imagining what he would be doing. However, the extraordinary thing is that you seem to think far less about family than you would have imagined. I feel I would have been much more occupied with them if Victoria was not with me. She seemed to fill the gap, so when going to out of the way places, take your daughter!

There were only ten people in the whole world further North than us: The Dutch Expedition and Pen and the five with whom he is walking the last degree. I found that thinking of this made me realise just how far from civilisation we were, and how lucky we were to be able to take part in a genuine wilderness expedition.

*

Victoria:

We walked for eight hours and I really felt that we had covered good distance, only to discover that we had covered only seven miles.

Whereas you make excellent time on the flat pans, just one tiny pressure ridge, only twenty yards wide, can take nearly half an hour to cross, which significantly reduces your average speed. We had lots of flat pans but the snow was very heavy, which slowed us down. We came across a wonderful lead where we just glided along, it really was like pulling a feather. We all prayed for more like that and preferably heading North. I felt good for most of the day but by the end of eight hours was knackered.

Mum and I tended to walk at the back, with Paula and Lynne at the front. It works well like that, and meant that Mum and I could keep an eye on each other when crossing leads. We were very protective of each other, I just kept thinking what Dad would say if anything happened to Mum.

My thoughts were starting to get more in depth when I walked, now that the initial novelty of a pressure ridge or lead had worn off. I spent hours analysing my job and my love life, getting more and more confused all the time. Walking in the Arctic was like going on a retreat, you walk for a whole day without really talking to anyone else, so you have unlimited time to really think without being distracted by other people, the telephone, overdue bills etc. It was almost a cleansing experience. The only problem with walking along in my own world was that when the person in front of me stopped I would not notice until too late, and would promptly fall head first over my skis as I crashed into their sledge.

*

Tuesday 15th April

Sue:

We woke up to a sea mist all over the place and a cold wind. We had rather a slow start, but after about one and a half hours we suddenly found a series of frozen leads going North. They led to an area of blue ice - electric blue, in great lumps, up to twenty foot high. They were in straight lines, almost like roads or fields with dry stone walls. We all felt we had walked at least eight miles, but in fact it was only six and a half. It was a really marvellous day, stunning sights, some of the things we saw are impossible to describe.

It is an incredible dream world. On the flat pans you get the effect of rippling waves, rather like ripples of sand in the desert, but it is the sea. Sometimes the drifting snow blows and swirls around you so that it is like a sandstorm in the desert. Some pans have very large sastrugi, these are wind-blown snow ridges that then freeze, and can slow you up quite considerably. Sometimes when the pressure ridges have been thrust up the ice sinks and water comes up, which can then be covered by blown snow. This is something to be careful of, as you do not realise there is water underneath and there is a danger of getting your feet wet. The water seems to form little ponds in other areas. Sometimes it is still wet and shines in the sun, other times it has begun to freeze and the ice crystals are forming.

We began to get an idea of ice and the different thicknesses and approximate age. When we came across frozen leads we moved very fast, but unfortunately not many seemed to run North/South. Victoria took me down a vast pile of frozen ice cubes, coming down it on skis - exciting beyond measure. I felt about ten years old playing follow my leader. But we do have to be careful of the skis, as we have no spare ones. The question is always: do you take them off to climb a ridge, which is quicker; but then you have to take your gloves off to take the skis off and fix them to the sledge, and when you have got to the other side it is the same in reverse. This can take up to five minutes to achieve, and your fingers get fumblier when trying to put the skis back on.

Our tent life is very cheerful; once inside any bad moments of the day are forgotten. Denise makes us laugh, as when she opens the tent and says 'I'm going to the bathroom' - we all wonder - what bathroom? Going out to the loo last thing at night, wearing just thermals and our slippers, it is not as one would have imagined it, i.e. pee freezing in mid stream! The crap flap works well too. This had been my major worry, how would one cope with the lack of privacy, but in the Arctic you really do not mind. Everyone has got the same problems as you, and it is incredible how you lose your inhibitions. Once you have 'let go' you realise that privacy is something that you can learn to live without. Having said that, I would not like to lose it for too long a period, but it is something that can be done without for a time. This was yet another lesson for a fifty something in a rut! Loos are nice, but there are other things that are more important.

Vapour barrier liners seemed to rule our lives, in bed, in our boots and I used them in my gloves to prevent the sweat wetting my outer layers. It always seemed to take just under three hours from breakfast till we left. We spent the whole time boiling billies (kettles), and found that we were drinking more each day. The Arctic has a very dry atmosphere, which seems odd as it is the sea, but the intense cold seems to drive away any moisture. This would be a good place for those who suffer from rheumatism! I found that all aches and pains had disappeared. We all felt by now that we had settled into a routine, but always with the goal of heading North.

We got quite used to eating frozen salami and Parma ham - luckily none of us had problems with our teeth - but I found so much sweet stuff not so good. I am not a chocoholic and felt that the one item of food I would die for would be a cream cracker. But it is extraordinary how quickly you get used to the butter mixed in with the cereal , I found that it being frozen made it easier to eat.

We felt we were a good team and Matty and Denise had begun to unwind. I think that Denise was totally focussed on the Pole, while Matty was more laid back about it. She was quite a private person and we were only just beginning to feel we were getting to know her, but both of them gave us great confidence. For them it was just as much an adventure, as neither had attempted the Pole before. Denise was someone that I liked a lot. She took less getting to know, was always cheerful, always positive and had a great sense of rather ironical humour. Matty also had a good sense of humour, but was more of a dreamer than Denise.

✟

Victoria:

We skied from 9.30 am to 5.40 pm. We had a wonderful lead for two hours and felt we had made really good mileage, then we followed this amazing "wall" for ages. It really was like walking in a field along a dry stone wall. In the tent we all had bets on what the mileage would be, and were very disappointed to find that it was only six miles. However, we had had some quite rough terrain.

I loved finding alternative routes when getting over the rubble. I am a very analytical person and I would stand and look at the options for a few seconds before crossing. If I had chosen a good route the satisfaction was immense, but I got so angry with myself if it was a bad route, ie if the sledge got stuck and tipped over. It did not matter how perfectly you had packed your sledge, they are just like photocopiers: the more angry you get, the more they go wrong. Talking to them nicely, and taking a deep breath before starting again is the only solution!

Everyone was becoming far more relaxed in the tent, mainly because we all knew the routine by this stage. Lynne and Mum had an ongoing 'discussion' about field sports, while Matty was coming out with more of her wonderful quotes: "You can tell when it is time for a break because you are warm". This was a slight exaggeration, but after stopping for a break it could often take up to half an hour before your fingers finally got warm again. It really was so important not to sweat, as even stopping for one minute led to your body temperature dropping very fast.

*

Internet Report

McVitie's Penguin Polar Relay - Update 15 April 1997. More reports:

Penguin Charlie are getting into their paces now. This evening after their fourth day on the ice they are at 85degs36minsN 73degs52minsW, having basically achieved an average of just over six nautical miles a day, not bad given the heavy sledges.

One of the issues for the ice team in recent days has been drift - namely the movement of the ice on which they are walking, the best comparison being a moving carpet. The ice team get a feel for this most acutely when they check their position every morning with the GPS and ascertain how much and in which direction they have drifted overnight. A drift of nearly a mile is not uncommon. When translated into mph over the 12 hours or so they are camped, this is approximately 0.1mph. It may not seem a lot, but when the drift is southwards it is not something you want to learn first thing in the morning when you are faced with another hard day's slog North.

The drift most commonly experienced seems to have been to the East. This is in common with the other expeditions out on the ice. All of them started out from Ward Hunt along the 75th longitude. They have now all shifted over to the East to the 72nd and 73rd degree of longitude. In fact the distance between the degrees of longitude at about the 85th/86th latitude, while being significant, is not that great i.e. about four miles. The problem for the teams on the ice is to decide whether to counter the easterly drift by walking due North Northwest (say) every day, or whether to keep heading exactly due North every day, in the belief that the consistent easterly drift of one week will be balanced out in future weeks by a consistent westerly drift.

In other parts of the Arctic Ocean there do appear to be consistent drifts of the ice, brought on by known oceanic currents. With respect to the "track" leading from Ward Hunt up to the Pole there does not appear to be any consistent current over weeks. Indeed this is one of the reasons that expeditions leave from Ward Hunt Island rather than from points closer to the Pole such as the northernmost tip of Greenland, where there are apparently some much stronger currents which can have some very significant adverse southerly direction in them.

If there is any one out there who can shed some greater light onto this debate then we would be pleased to hear from you.

So much for the technical stuff, and back to softer issues more relevant to the MPPR; there was a rather moving meeting in the tiny Resolute airport building tonight between the outgoing Bravo team and the incoming Delta team. The former with a twinkle in their eye full of the "I've just done it" confidence, and the latter with an excited but apprehensive look about them. The meeting stopped others in the airport in their tracks. Everyone basically just gawped at this rather striking band of women, looking quite the part in their sponsor badged clothing, exchanging stories rapidly.

Penguin Delta comprising Andre Chadwick (sister of Steve, the creator of the website), Juliette May, Sarah Jones and Rosie Stancer start their training tomorrow. Good luck to them.

151 miles gone, 264 to go. **End.**

*

Wednesday 16th April
Sue:

I got up very cold this morning. During the night I had become very hot, sweated like mad, then got very cold. Getting out of bed was awful. I longed for someone to say 'poor you' and show a little sympathy! But after lighting the fires and making some tea I soon felt better and warmed up. When you are out on the ice there is no time to feel sorry for yourself. I did find, though, that I was always conscious of being the oldest, and as such, felt that I must not show any signs of what could be construed as old age! I was always aware that Victoria was keeping an eye on me, and that was quite comforting. I did not want the others to feel that having an older person would delay or inhibit them. Generally, however, I did not feel my age, and in fact, because of the fun of each day, felt considerably younger than I actually was!

We had a record breaking day - nine miles in nine hours. We all felt in very good order, and when Matty suggested another hour, our ninth, we all said go for it. The conditions were not too bad, mostly flat pans which we seemed to fly across. There were more of the incredibly blue ice chunks. Each successive day did not diminish one's wonder at the Arctic scenery.

When going across the flat boring bits you need to think of something, so I either recited poetry or hymns to myself, or imagined climbing the Brown Clee, Ben Lawers or Schiehallion. I could visualise every footstep, but particularly the colours. Fairly frequently your mind got distracted by an obstacle that you had to go round or climb over, but I found that I could pick up where I left off. Sometimes it took the whole day to go up one hill, but I was totally immersed in this imaginary world, which is strange, because it was the real one! Other times I tried to imagine what Jeremy, Philip or Edward would be doing at that precise moment. Pattingham seemed so far away, but it was very comforting to think about life going on perfectly normally there, the chickens being fed, the pony exercised or the dogs going for a walk.

Sometimes the feeling of space was such that you almost felt lost in it. It could be very austere and the ice can give out such coldness. Rather like the land on Ellesmere, the North is unyielding and can be unforgiving of mistakes. The very frigidness of the beauty can inspire fear, but I think that because we all got on with each other and supported each other, the fearful side of the Arctic was reduced.

*

Victoria:

We skied from 9.15 am - 6.15 pm and had a record day in both hours and miles. We were all on an absolute high in the evening and to top it off we had Ben's Bean Feast for dinner, totally disgusting! Mum's bindings snapped but we managed to repair them vaguely, as we had not taken spare bindings to save weight. It is amazing how ingenious one becomes when there are limited resources available to mend something.

My passion for maths has finally turned out to be useful. When I had exhausted my thoughts on men and work whilst walking, I turned to maths. I would give myself a number, say 2436, and using only the numbers, 2,3,4 I had to add, subtract, divide and multiply until I got there. It was quite difficult to begin with as my brain was not used to storing lots of numbers, I tended to write everything down or use computers. However after a few days I had this down to a fine art, and as far as Mum was concerned if it kept me quiet then great!

Whilst walking I found that my imagination would run wild. I was brought up reading Babar the Elephant books and most days I would see ice which looked identical to Babar or his wife Celeste. Lynne swore that she could see her children sometimes in the ice. Speaking as a totally unartistic person, I was almost inspired to stop and sketch the shapes; perhaps it was just as well that I did not!

We would radio in to base camp every other night and we all took it in turns to do the radio. This was something that I loved doing, it probably stemmed from my days in the OTC at university. Talking to the outside world on the radio really did make us realise how lonely it must have been for the original Arctic explorers. Not only were they often away for years, unsure of where they were actually heading off to, but they had virtually no contact with the outside world, apart from an occasional Inuit. It must have been very frightening and desperate at times.

Our rations were all very carefully calculated, and even if we were not hungry it was very important that we actually ate our full daily allowance. Like Mum I was not a particularly big chocolate eater, with the exception of Cadbury's Creme Eggs (which taste delicious when frozen), so I had to find a way to somehow eat copious amounts of chocolate. Hence I became addicted to a cup of hot chocolate with at least four or five pieces of chocolate melted in it. Quite yummy, especially when you get to the gooey bit at the bottom! The only downside was that when it came to cleaning my teeth the 'water' in my mug tended to have a slightly chocolatey flavour as I never got to actually clean the mug out properly.

The worst part of the day was the first five minutes. Matty would call out 'Rise and Shine' and we knew that we had to get out of our nice warm sleeping bags, put on ice encrusted suits, somehow stagger outside and undo our crap flaps while our fingers were still numb from the cold. Having said that, once we had completed our morning ritual life got much better very quickly. The stoves would be on and a hot drink was followed by a large bowl of cereal, the same one every day! The only other truly bad moment was when we first put on our harnesses in the morning. Our back and hips would still ache from the previous day, and as we took the first step we would wonder once again what on earth we were doing there, and what fresh excitement and drama this new day might bring....

Chapter Seven

DIARIES: Stepping In!

Thursday 17th April

Sue:

Another record breaking day; nine miles again in only eight and a quarter hours. Morale was very good and we felt that we were well on our way to achieving a distance of over one hundred miles during our leg. Again we had more flat pans, I now began to find that my mind went into an automatic trance when these flat areas appeared in front of us. In the distance were always the icy blue ridges bounding the edge of our world; they seemed to stretch for miles, but actually we had no idea of the real distance. Rather like distant hills they were always a pale blue, the shadows being the only way that you could get some idea of scale.

The evening before, Denise had had a radio message saying that her first boyfriend had died of cancer. It was not unexpected but it was a very lonely place to hear bad news. In the afternoon we had a long talk about it while waiting for Lynne and Paula to cross a ridge, and for Victoria to do a Radio Four recording of the sound of ice. Sometimes on the ice you can have very private moments, when suddenly you forget that there are five other people out there.

When we did the washing up, only a tiny splodge of hot water and the wooden spoon was needed to clean the saucepan. The whole time we cooked, our clothes hung there on the lines drying above the stoves. We shared the toothpaste, melted by being kept in Victoria's underwear. Matty and Denise often peed in the night, and as my sleeping bag was the one by the door with the space beside it I got to hear them, rather smelly also, you could tell which one has done it by the smell. Ammonia for Matty! One of our worries was constipation, but the cereal seemed to work wonders, everyone went off at the same intervals before and after breakfast. We used snow wedges instead of loo paper, much more convenient and probably far more hygienic. I felt a bit like a dog looking for a place to go, you kicked a hole, performed, use the wedges to cover it up, and away you go. In the morning outside the tent it always looked as if there had been dozens of dogs visiting in the night, with all the pee places, no one went very far to do it! Whatever happens, I seemed to sleep incredibly well; into bed, two or three minutes and I was asleep, whatever the conditions.

We used the GPS for giving our exact position in the evening, but during the day we used the sun for navigation, together with our watches. At midday, for example, our shadow would be due North, at 6.00 pm it would be due East. Only when you couldn't see the sun did you use a compass, but it was incredibly sluggish, we were 91° out. The sun never got really high in the sky and it never set; neither did it get very low, it just went round at the same height day and night, but even at midnight it was always there. Despite the fact that we all went to bed in full sunlight none of us had a problem sleeping. The sun seemed to give out very little heat, but its movement was the only event that gave any idea of the passage of time. It was always a slightly strange light, not very bright, almost like the sort of sun you get at home in October or March.

*

Victoria:

A day from hell, I was not a happy bunny and just could not get

142

into it. Even though I knew that I was very lucky to be in the Arctic, my mind was not with it. We did however have excellent terrain with a few bumps to break the monotony. As a result we had another record day and covered nine miles. Morale was therefore very high.

We all felt very clean compared to when we had been training, but Matty and Denise were very keen on a daily strip wash regardless of how tired we all were, or how cold it was. It did help, not just hygienically but we felt much better mentally if we were clean(ish!). Talk in the tent definitely had hit an all time low. Put a group of women together, anywhere, and the conversation will eventually turn to men and sex. I am sure the same applies to men. We had a very funny evening discussing the boys back at base - Nobby, Mike and Geoff. Later on we spoke to Penguin Delta who had just arrived in Resolute. Rosie came on, sounding the same as ever, on a high! While doing my daily diary recording for Radio 4, Matty recorded twenty 'ums' No wonder I am an 'Arctic explorer' and not a foreign correspondent, my life long ambition.

*

Internet report

McVitie's Penguin Polar Relay - Update 17 April 1997. More reports:

Penguin Charlie have reported improving ice conditions over the last few days. To prove their point they have been clocking up some excellent progress - nine miles yesterday and the same again today. Tonight Charlie are at 85degs54minsN 73degs51minsW, leaving them 246 miles to go, 169 miles gone. **End.**

*

143

Friday 18ᵗʰ April

Sue:

When we woke up we found that we had drifted east six miles, so the day was spent walking almost due west. It was a good day, but I felt quite tired by the last hour. Each evening we guessed how many miles we had walked, and it was very depressing to find that we had walked far less than we thought.

We ate our breakfast and mended our equipment each morning. We washed our bodies and ate all our food out of the same bowl, but you got used to it. The only problem was the fact that it became increasingly difficult to get the grease out of the bowl; scouring with ice helped a little, but there was always a residue. Perhaps this layer of fat in our washing water helped protect our skins! I even got to the stage of conserving water by wetting my toothbrush in the tea before doing my teeth - lapsang flavoured toothpaste could perhaps become a fad of the future.

During the morning I had a long think about what I wanted to do with myself when I got back home. Suddenly I realised that there were so many things out there that I would like to do. But how could I balance achieving what I wanted to do with being happily married and not wanting to upset Jeremy? The start would be an Arts Foundation Course with the Open University. I have always wanted to do a degree, but had no idea in what subject. This would give me a taster in a variety of subjects and shake up my brain, which I was worried might have gone to sleep in the past thirty years!

I found the most difficult thing was getting out of the tent. I do not bend in the middle, and as the door was virtually at ground level, a round hole with a drawstring through it, quite a serious amount of

144

bending was required. I found the easiest way to get out was to crawl, the others just seemed to be able to walk out. Going outside, for however short a time, was always something of an effort. You had to be almost fully dressed and always needed gloves. I did find that the cold air stimulated you though, it was very invigorating.

Were we getting used to the amazing sights? Matty and I both thought that it was a kind of Hobbit/Middle World/Lord of the Rings type place in shades of white. We could get very contemplative when walking in our little worlds, wrapped up in our own thoughts! Because the ice was never ending, I felt that artists would love it, the incredible light and space. Matty and I discussed how we would paint it, and what colours we would use to get the shades of blue and white. But one still felt that the ice was implacable. However beautiful you find it, it has to be fought on its own terms.

It was an incredibly serene place sometimes. You walked in your own little world, the sun shone, the snow sparkled and you felt in a capsule, nothing existed outside your bright red suit. You thought, or tried to, but your brain did not let you concentrate for more than about a minute, then you somehow got distracted. You could be on another planet as nothing was quite what it seemed. We kept talking as if it was land.

Digging snow blocks became an enjoyable part of the day. Lynne and I would put on our duvet jackets, dig, then when we knelt down to pick up the blocks we would have a gossip; it was quite a relaxing time. We put them into stuff sacks and dinner bags, piled them outside the tent, and then came in to the hot soup, wonderful. At the end of the day it was a good feeling to be relaxing, chatting, sitting back, just thinking. We passed the stove round to each other to dry our feet. That evening Victoria

145

gave carriage driving lessons to Matty with webbing and we discovered she had done it when living in the States. We showed her how we used the reins, suddenly it brought home very close.

One of the real problems during the day was keeping the cameras operating, as the batteries did not last for long in the cold. We had to keep them in plastic bags down our fronts, next to the skin, it was very cold. Paula did the team video and the camera only worked for about four minutes at a time.

We were usually in bed by 8.30 pm, listening to Denise if it was a day for radioing in. It was very comforting listening to the call when tucked up in bed - all warm with the hot water bottles by our feet - gorgeous! It was like listening to a bed time story. The best time in the tent was when it was your turn for the collapsible chair, and you were not doing the food or water. You tucked the hot water bottles under your suit, one at your back and one at your front, the suit steamed a bit, but began to dry off and the only thing missing was a glass of whisky.

*

Victoria:

Had an OK day, very sunny and windy. The terrain was flat but the snow seemed very slow and sure enough we only covered eight miles. However the best news of all was that we crossed the 86th parallel. It was like reaching a goal, or passing an exam. Arctic travel is about reaching the 90th and to cross yet another line of latitude off the list was a wonderful feeling. We really felt that we could make the 87th, our own personal goal, and were therefore asking for a changeover on the Saturday to give us maximum time possible.

We had a very funny evening discussing carriage driving with

146

Matty. I had to teach her how to hold the reins etc. as she had forgotten. She had been brought up driving as a child. I suppose that there are some similarities between dog sledding and carriage driving.

To see the midnight sun is such a surreal experience, if you look north you can see the sun, and if you look south you can see the moon. It is like being in some alien world and defies everything that you were ever taught at school: sun during the day and moon during the night.

Next morning we woke up to horrible weather and yet more drift east. As I lay in my bed I rather hoped that it would be a storm day. Suddenly there was a massive crack of ice, just the same as lightning, but much louder and closer. I was terrified, what on earth was I doing in this frightening place? At that precise moment I just wanted an aeroplane. The Arctic is like that though, your emotions change by the minute. One second you cannot believe that you are in such a beautiful place, and the next you are frightened out of your skin.

I spent the day writing my letter of resignation in my head, I was dreading having to give it in, partly because I knew that while teaching was the career path I wanted to follow, I was giving up a well paid job and a lifestyle that went with it. However I had realised that working with young children was something I was good at and had always enjoyed. Life is too short to put ideas on hold, so it was time to pursue this idea.

*

Saturday 19th April

Sue:

We drifted two and a half nautical miles east, back to where we had been the day before. We seemed to be drifting more and more and it was like living on a treadmill. It began to get somewhat depressing, we were putting an enormous amount of energy into covering as much ground as possible, only to find that each time we went to bed the sea gained back the ground that we had covered the day before. During the day we walked five miles, but even as we were doing this we still drifted three miles to the east. This is where you have to say to yourself that your aim is to get to the Pole, and every little inch gained is an advantage. You cannot let yourself become depressed because of the drift.

Even though you are part of a group of people there is always a feeling of isolation when you are walking. It was not the real world. I found it hard to comprehend that I could not pinpoint precisely where I was in the world, I was floating on the sea.

In the morning we came across a very rubbery lead. You could see the waves lapping gently at the side, but one had to keep moving, and not follow in someone else's tracks as this would have weakened the ice. The water looked black, black, black, almost sinister. I had to remind myself that it was about two and a half miles deep here. I did not like Victoria being behind me, nor she me, so we had to take it in turns, particularly over the rubber ice. It started getting very windy, gusting up to 35 mph. It was not very cold, only -29^{0}C, but the wind chill made it feel worse. The spindrift was blowing, it was all very photogenic, and looked lovely, but you could not see very far. Because of the wind getting up, and the drift snow blowing, we decided to stop early; the weather seemed

148

to be changing.

As we approached each ridge we had a one track mind: how do I get up, which is the best way, how can I get my sledge up, can I stop it jamming? We helped each other push and pull our sledges - Lynne got run over by hers one day, which did shake her. Sometimes when we came to ridges the sledges slipped, and then you needed all your strength to keep them up and stop them tipping over. Once over the top you had to be sure that they did not bang down too heavily on the other side, or they might break. But sometimes they did come down with a hell of a crack, and we wondered why the fibreglass did not shatter. When we met an obstacle they stopped with a such a huge jerk that we nearly fell over, because of the unexpectedness of this sudden halt. Life is never smooth going for a sledge.

We always camped on multi-year ice, it was less likely to split under us - marvellous! Also there seems to be more snow on multi-year, which is what we drank. You have to be careful not to get salt ice, otherwise you are drinking salt water. It only snows about two inches in the Arctic each year, a worse drought than the Sahara, so the snow we were drinking could have been hundreds of years old. It was certainly very pleasant drink - no pollution, no chlorine or additives in the water.

We had to wear goggles the whole time, partly because of snow blindness and also to protect our faces. Every halt we looked at each other to check for frostnip. I looked at Victoria's during one halt and said she looked fine; luckily Paula looked too, because as I had got my goggles on I could not see the beginning of frostnip. She was all right, and just rubbed it and it disappeared, but it could have been very nasty if it had gone unnoticed. Our skins seemed to stay in very good condition, but we

149

did all smear on our Neutrogena face cream night and morning!

Each morning we buried the fuel cans where they would probably sink in the summer. If we had taken them back to Resolute they would be thrown into the sea just the same, so we were really better off disposing of them on our way. It did worry us though, littering up the Arctic, but, unlike in the Antarctic, a metal fuel can will be worn away by rust eventually. We had decided to take more fuel than most expeditions, so that we could be warm and dry our clothes; it was definitely worth it and not a problem pulling the extra load.

We always woke up feeling optimistic in the morning, hoping that we had not moved too much towards Greenland during the night. A good night's sleep does help the spirits. It was incredible how six women can live in such a tiny space and get on so well together. Sometimes we became quite weak with laughter, usually over something incredibly silly!

*

Victoria:

Well, it was a day to remember. The wind was very gusty all day from the SW and we finally hit all the rubble and ridges that Kono had talked about on the radio. We set out and within five minutes had to take off our skis, a bad start. From then on it just got worse and it was skis on and skis off and even a fair bit of walking. It was so windy that poor Paula managed to pee everywhere but on the snow! As a result of the strong winds the easterly drift is massive We drifted two or three miles east, despite walking due west and just during supper we drifted a further one mile east. This was a major problem; if we carried on we would get to Greenland, therefore our aim was now to reach the 75th longitude, never mind the 87th latitude! It was like walking on a treadmill. We just slid more than we could walk, Lynne reckoned that we should try running!

I had a good day despite the weather and was 8-9/10 all day. Mum drove me bonkers when she always said 9-10/10 rather than 0-10/10. As an eternal optimist her scale was very different, and this would often get the rest of us down, as we felt like wimps for saying 5/10 when Mum would say 9/10 again. I felt as if the wind was about to blow the tent away. It was flapping wildly, and all our clothes on the washing line were waving about furiously. However when the snow was blowing across the ground it looked just like a desert sand storm. I kept on having visions of Ralph Fiennes in *The English Patient* coming around the next corner!

Going out of the tent for a pee on a nice day was bad enough, but when it was so cold and windy, you hardly dared go outside. The effort required was amazing: put gloves and hat on, run out in thermals (quite a sight) with 'slippers'/boots, check direction of wind, squat, snow wedge, run back, undress and warm up. Wow!! With practice this can be done in two to three minutes!!

Lying in my sleeping bag I realised how lucky we were and that no one would ever understand what it is like unless they have been here, but at that precise moment all I wanted was a bottle of Chardonnay and a plate of hot new potatoes and Greek salad. It is amazing what you fantasise about. I would regularly go shopping at Sainsbury's while walking along, and was able to taste and touch everything I put in my trolley. I began to wonder if I had gone totally mad, but apparently the others had similar thoughts.

*

Internet report

McVitie's Penguin Polar Relay - Update 19th April 1997. More reports:

Yesterday another degree was knocked off the seven required for the Penguin Relay to get to the Pole (from 83 degrees to 90 degrees). This is fantastic news and it means that each team has had the satisfaction of crossing a degree line. Alpha went through the 84th, Bravo the 85th and now Charlie the 86th.

Penguin Charlie radioed in this evening and were congratulated on their achievement. They reported continued drift, generally to the East, and increasing wind speeds. These winds are currently affecting a large area. This evening we had reported to us that heavy winds were hampering the progress of an expedition which is near the Pole, and certainly here in Resolute the wind has been strong for a number of days, making life difficult due to large snowdrifts.

Tonight the team are camped at 86degs 6minsN, 72deg20minsE at a temperature of -24 deg C, leaving 234 miles to go with 181 behind them.**End.**

*

Sunday 20ᵗʰ April
Sue:

We drifted ten and a half miles east during the night, it was very depressing. We stayed in bed until 11 am, when Matty and Denise had to go out and dig out the sides of the tent as the seams were straining - it was quite a worry lying there listening to the ski tent pole wobbling around;

and what would we do if it blew away, build igloos or what? We heard the ice moving during the night, we could not see it but the sound is like a tube train coming out of a tunnel. Lying in bed I had realised, (not that I had not thought about it before) that we were up against life and death situations; if things go wrong they could go VERY wrong. We were worried about how many days the wind might blow for, would the tent stand up to the wind, would we (when the time came) find a landing strip, or would there be too many leads? Lying in bed was not conducive to happy thoughts, but it did conserve energy and save fuel. It was -20^0C, not that cold, but because of the wind chill it felt in fact very cold. Denise said there was no point in going out in weather like this, as you only got frost bite and then worse. The secret, in bad weather, is to keep dry - wet is the biggest killer, whether sweat or water. Despite the storm, when we had the cookers going we all felt very secure.

Victoria spent the morning separating fruit from nuts. I did the same later on. We fried pancetta and Parma ham for lunch - it was salty, but very nice. Freshly made chocolate biscuit cake for tea, thanks to Victoria. (Our shortbread, butter and chocolate rations melted and mixed together!) I think we all over ate and felt a bit sick. We read our books, Paula: Nick Hornby, Lynne: Joanna Trollope, Victoria: Robert Goddard, and me: The Bible. I read three books, it is the way to read it as opposed to listening to lessons in church. It meant more here too, away from home and help. Perhaps you feel closer to God as it is a new and unspoilt world and there is no pollution. Your senses are definitely sharpened up and much more acute and I think this was why we all felt so lucky to be here. It was wonderful to be part of a team, but still to have to be reliant on yourself.

By now we had even moved a time zone east. Twenty two miles altogether, but after the rest we should be able to make up the time and slippage because we all feel that the rest has boosted up our batteries, both mental and physical.

*

Victoria:

A very gusty night, at times the wind was blowing at 40 mph. Denise woke me up when she did the radio and I had a very funny message from a group of friends from home - obviously made up after a few beers. I wondered how many people had heard this slightly risque message going out over the airwaves!

Woke up to even more appalling winds and the sounds of Denise and Matty digging the tent out of snow drifts. Visibility was very poor so we spent the day in the tent which at times was incredibly frustrating, but in some ways it was quite nice to have a rest. We stayed in bed until 11.00am, half dozing and half awake. It was so windy during the night that we all had to pee in the tent, rather than brave the outdoors. This having vowed that we would never lower ourselves to such standards! At various intervals during the day I honestly thought that the tent would take off. It really was quite scary - in the middle of the Arctic protected only by a flimsy bit of canvas. I did feel slightly unnerved by the whole thing. We eventually got up, Paula and my sleeping bags had snow all over them from the hole in the roof, and we looked like snowmen.

The morning was spent cooking, the Parma ham smelt delicious as it was being fried, but was so salty we could only manage one mouthful each. I spent hours separating all my dried fruit from the peanuts - little things please little minds - but we were going to soak all the fruit in Paula's brandy in an attempt to make Arctic Christmas Pudding. It did not quite work unfortunately, however the highlight of our cooking was chocolate biscuit cake - a top restaurant could not have made it taste any more delicious.

Paula and I went on top of the ridge behind the tent to do some filming; it was freezing and we nearly got blown away by the wind. The east drift was by now extremely serious, we had moved ten miles in twenty four hours. I felt that we should change the expedition goal and be the first British women to walk to Greenland.

*

Monday 21st April

Sue:

WHAT A DAY

It started off as a normal Arctic day, a very flat light and weak sun. We had floated six miles during the night and had a four and a half mile drift east. It was rather a misty sort of day, the sun eventually just about disappeared, but because of the lack of sun the ice appears bluer, a diffused light. There were rubble pans, then some semi-frozen leads, all right to cross quickly, but the ice was soft. After about five hours we came to more and more open water, which caused a sea mist to form because the sea is warmer than the air, about.-2^0C. Matty crossed a frozen lead, it was softish ice, but OK to cross. A sort of solid slush, a kind of jumble of ice chunks held together by the ice floes on each side, both of which were fairly large. Very much the kind of frozen lead that we had crossed countless times before without a second thought.

I was behind Denise, when suddenly Matty said, 'it's moving, go, go, go'. Black water appeared on the bank on her side, suddenly I was in. My skis were not on the ice any longer but in the Arctic. Every lump of ice I got hold of broke, but I did not feel it was me, because you are trying to save yourself you do not think of the danger, it is just survival - but swimming in skis was quite difficult! Then I found a small floater. By now my boot and ski had come off, so I climbed on board. The floater then disintegrated under me ... so another swim. Then I found a bigger one, which was only the size of a very small kitchen table and felt distinctly wobbly. Strangely enough the sea did not feel as cold as you would have thought. By now the lead was quite big and seemed to be getting still larger. I was still attached to my pulk, which was probably a good thing.

Victoria at this stage was swimming too. She had fallen in trying to rescue me, thinking that Jeremy would be furious if anything happened to me! She managed to find a bigger floater than mine. She suddenly asked me to throw her my camera, I thought she was being kind and rescuing my film. Not a bit, she took a photograph! She then got hold of my pulk rope and pulled my floater to her lump of ice. I crawled across, having removed my remaining ski, feeling rather idiotic with one boot and one thin M & S cotton sock. I was very worried about frostbite by this stage. The extraordinary thing was that I did not feel cold. I was wet up to my neck (and now realised why they had tested our swimming during the selection weekend), but because my body was so warm when I fell in, the heat had remained. So, for those who think you die after one minute in the frozen Arctic, you do not!

Matty then threw a line to us, Victoria caught it, and she pulled us in. However there was an overhang on her bank, so we had to put my pulk between Victoria's floater and the bank. We stood on the pulk and got out onto dry land (even at this stage we refer to the ice as land, it is the mental conditioning: because it felt safe it was land in our minds.)

Meanwhile Denise had also fallen in while trying to rescue equipment. She swam to the other bank, great high banks of ice, and Paula and Lynne pulled her out. However they were separated from us by an ever growing expanse of water. Denise was wonderful, Victoria said she was like a terrier rescuing the equipment She would not give up until she was either exhausted or had recovered it all.

So on our side we had just two pulks, the cookers, a radio, but no tent. We rolled in the snow which helped absorb some of the moisture out of our suits. Matty put my bare foot on her bare bosom, which warmed the foot, but not Matty. The foot was not white, which was good news, it just looked bruised. I was just relieved that it was not my nose, and Matty a man, because if it had been, it would have been nose down in the crotch....A chap's warmest place?! Luckily we had a down jacket in each sledge, so we put them on, on top of our wet clothes, as without a tent there was no way of getting dry. We shouted to the others, who had put up the tent in order to change Denise's wet clothes and prevent potential hypothermia, that we would walk north and would try to find a way round the lead to join them, and could they start walking too when they had dried Denise.

I was missing a boot as it had drifted to the other side, so put a spare liner and a stuff sack on. It was very difficult to walk without skis, I kept falling over, but it did warm me up so I was only cold for a short time. We walked round a huge area of water, then found a semi-island,

157

which we went on to look for the others. The visibility was not at all good and most of the time we could not see them. There was still no way across, so we shouted that we would keep going north. Having turned round we retraced our footsteps only to find that the semi-island was in the process of becoming a real island. I did find it quite frightening to realise that everything around us was in a state of continuous movement. We only just got across.

By now we were both feeling quite warm. I was pulling my pulk which helped, but we only had three poles between us. We were still walking north, worried that there would be more leads on the other side and that they would keep splitting like a Y with us and the others moving further and further apart. We came to a lead and a real miracle happened. I was wondering how we were going to get out of this situation, so I had just sent up a quick prayer, not thinking it would be answered quite so instantly (which made me very glad I read the Bible the previous night). At that moment we heard 'the tube train coming out of the tunnel' noise in the distance and saw the current in our lead moving fast, then I noticed the two sides were moving together, just the little area where we were standing, and within the space of one minute one hundred foot of open water closed up. Across we went and there we were, on the other side, (to begin with the others did not believe me that the ice was moving, they thought I was hallucinating).

It all happened so fast that we barely had time to actually realise what was taking place. What was the most incredible fact was that about an hour later the lead split apart again and was much wider. A true miracle. And there were the others, ten minutes away, having only just got the tent down, and very glad to see us. They were in a rather unsafe place, a tiny

158

island formed from ice chunks which was beginning to split away from the piece we were on. We moved back onto the smooth ice, and set up tent, and changed into dry things. The infuriating thing was that that morning I had put on clean underwear and spare gloves, which meant that I would have to put the dirty ones on again. We had hot soup and cups of tea - wonderful.

Later the others went back and got the two boots and two skis, all that was now missing were six poles and we decided to try again in the morning for them. If we had not recovered the equipment the expedition would have been called off.

We had a really cheerful evening, and radioed in to base camp to tell them the full story. I do not think they realised what we were telling them to begin with, but reality soon sunk in. They then read out some faxes to us. Jeremy had sent one about the dogs, pony and how the bantams had just hatched two broods of chicks! However garbled they were it was marvellous to have the messages; the everyday happenings after a day such as we had just had made the real world seem closer, and helped us to realise that even if we were not at home, life was continuing as usual - when you are away it is the little things that really count.

*

Victoria:

I woke up at 6.00 am wishing it was another storm day. The constant walking due west in order to compensate for our easterly drift was starting to get me down. So much for us reaching the 87th or making one hundred miles. The weather closed in and it got pretty snowy, with the flat light we could not see a thing. Paula and Lynne were at the back because they wanted a change of scenery, fate must have dealt them a hand. We came across a lead, part solid, part wobbly but it seemed fine. Matty crossed it and told us to spread out - the usual drill. Denise went on another route. I followed Mum, (because she is scared of leads she always goes first), and then suddenly my feet went in. I was slightly unnerved but more annoyed than anything else. I then turned to Paula and asked if she had got it on camera, as she was recording at the time. She had not but by pure chance proceeded to film the next ten minutes or so.

The next thing I knew was that Mum was in the water. I managed to unclip my pulk, as I had visions of it going into the water and pulling me down, and skied across to Mum. I started to haul her out of the water with her pulk line - she was in up to her shoulders - when my piece of ice disappeared from under me, and down I went. We then spent the next few minutes trying to get on to these ice islands. I likened it to trying to catch a beach ball in the sea, every time you got hold of it, it moved away from you. Eventually we were both on islands, but I began to get quite concerned about Mum. She was saying 'shit' all the time and had a funny look in her eyes, like when she is in a bad mood or not in control of a situation. We were both sat on our islands, Mum attached to her pulk and just a ski pole to help us. I had lost one boot and ski but rescued them and put the boot on and threw the ski towards Lynne and Paula. Mum had also lost her boot and ski. Matty chucked a rope and we managed to attach it to me. I then used the pulk and ski pole to pull Mum to me, and she came onto my island. Finally Matty pulled us in and using Mum's pulk we jumped onto land. Mum was terrified of jumping onto land, not surprising considering what she had just been through.

Meanwhile Denise had gone back to her side, fell in and then

160

went backwards and forwards, in and out, trying to collect all the lost equipment. Within ten minutes Matty, Mum, me, two pulks, five boots, three skis and three poles were on one side, and on the other side Paula, Lynne, Denise, four pulks, seven skis, five boots and three poles. i.e. we were missing two skis, one boot, six poles and one throw line.

Denise was very cold and wet so Lynne and Paula put up the tent and warmed her up. Matty meanwhile kept us warm, especially Mum's toes. We then put on our Parkas and wind trousers and set off to follow the lead until we could cross it, hoping that the others would follow us on the other side. We were very concerned as to what might happen if we did not meet up, as one side had a tent and radio and the other (us) had fuel and ARGOS. We walked along the lead trying various potential crossing points with the reality of how serious a situation we were in beginning to sink in. At one stage we were standing on the bank trying to see the others in case the leads split in a Y and we all went up the wrong one, when the banks of the lead just closed together. A total miracle. Mum had been waffling away about the ice moving, but Matty and I were ignoring her because it seemed as if she was just talking to herself. Suddenly I could hear a tube train, almost underneath my feet, and the ice just came together (it had been at least a hundred foot wide) in under a minute to form a ridge that we could cross.

Eventually we met up with the others and within half an hour had set up camp. I was definitely feeling very wobbly, partly because of what could have happened to Mum, and partly because I knew exactly what Dad would say when he found out. Matty and Denise were very calm once we were all out of the water, and Denise, Mum and I all said how it had made us feel much closer. Even the team as a whole became

161

much closer, having gone though something like that. Paula, Lynne and Matty went back later to retrieve the skis and boot, but could not rescue the poles. We had actually covered four miles before all the excitement. I felt so wobbly, but at the same time almost exhilarated. It really was life or death, and we lived. You laugh to hide the fear, but I knew that Dad would never forgive us, and I did not blame him. If something had happened to Mum I would have felt so guilty.

*

Internet report

McVitie's Penguin Polar Relay - Update 21 April 1997. More reports:

In the last update it was reported that Penguin Charlie were experiencing increasing winds, such as those hitting Resolute of late. This certainly proved to be the case not only for Penguin Charlie but for all the expeditions on the Arctic pack ice.

The increased winds caused the team to stay put yesterday. This enforced rest day was, it could be argued, no bad thing in view of the mileage that Charlie had been putting under their belt, although being in a tent for two nights and a day can become very frustrating. However the real issue is that the high winds are causing the pack ice to drift at up to 1 knot (1 nautical mile per hour)! Penguin Charlie experienced varying drift levels aggregating in an eastward movement from 72degs13minsW to 68degs54minsW, some 15miles, on their layover day. Fortunately it wasn't southwards, unlike a lone Japanese who having walked from the Russian side to within 11 miles of the Pole over recent weeks is reputed to have drifted back such that he is now a staggering 42 miles south of the Pole. Very depressing.

162

The weather forecast is for the wind to subside over the next couple of days and perhaps increase again from the west thereafter. It is therefore unlikely that the easterly drift will subside much prior to the intended Charlie/Delta changeover due on Friday 25th.

Penguin Delta are currently on their four day / three night final training session around Resolute. They have been subjected to the full force of the blizzard which has been blowing over the last couple of days. We look forward to their tales.

The ARGOS position tonight is 86 degrees10 minutesN 68 degrees 02 minutesW., 185 miles gone 230 to go. **End**

*

Tuesday 22nd April

Sue:

I slept fitfully and we were up at 6.30 am. After breakfast Paula, Denise and Matty went and recovered some of the lost ski poles. They secured Matty with all the pulk ropes, made a snow/ice bridge and she crept across the rather unstable ice and chipped free all the remaining equipment, which by now had floated to our side and was semi-frozen into the ice, so now we were only missing two poles. We decided that Victoria and I would share three between us, and Matty and Denise would also share three. The throw bag was also rescued, but one pole was too far out and one had disappeared.

Meanwhile we finished drying things. The night before we had put our suits outside to freeze dry them a little, which means shaking the ice off after an hour or two, but neither my suit nor Denise's were fully dry, so we wore trousers and windproof jackets. Salt water always takes longer to dry and stays sticky until it is.

We set off about 11.00 am and discovered we were on an island. On the east side was a huge expanse of open water like the River Tay in winter, and we walked the whole way round, starting off due North. There was even more water visible and our moving ice from the day before was well over half a mile across It was quite chilling to think of what had happened yesterday. Eventually, very near where the others had put their tent the day before, we found a way across. It was a bit nerve wracking. The ice was quite soft, and we realised everything was moving, I went first and helped pull the pulks up the other side. The day seemed to get worse, there were more and more leads.

At one stage, when Matty was on a frozen lead of ice chunks, Paula shouted: 'Get off, it's moving'. Matty jumped back, and at that moment the area in front of us started to go by in slow motion. The whole lead was like a slushy river of ice chunks, moving at a slow pace, then stopping, then continuing. It was grinding and groaning, and then it would go quiet again, meanwhile vast chunks of ice were being sucked down and pushed up, some the size of small lorries. Others the size of cars were being pushed up, ice 'land' was tilting and slipping, it was all very primeval, very scary indeed.

The extraordinary thing was that leads are not meant to flow, they usually just remain still, in theory we all drift at the same speed. It was like a frozen lava flow, inexorable and totally powerful. Supposing we had been half way across when it started moving. Paula managed to film some of the movement, but it was hard to capture and I do not think it is possible to explain the full effect to someone who has not seen it happening. We just stood there in silence watching it move past us. The large ice island on the other side moved gently south. Matty and Denise had never seen anything like this before. It was very unusual. We were lucky to have seen it.

Victoria was very down, in tears at the third halt. Lynne was good with her, I think that Paula saying she liked real excitement got Victoria upset. I did not like seeing her unhappy, but did not want to fuss her. I felt that my tummy was in a permanent state of butterflies, my mouth was dry and my heart went fast every time we came to another lead. I have never been so frightened, you just could not escape, you had to keep going north. I think that if we had not fallen in things would not have been so bad, but we kept thinking if we fall in again, can we survive twice?

Denise had taken the skins off her skis in the tent at breakfast, but at the first halt put them on again as there were some flat pans amongst all the moving ice. While she was doing this we climbed on top of the ridge to look where to go, but all you could see were small ice fields, huge ridges and miles of rubble, black water steaming, it was all very worrying. You felt that the ice was a living thing and you could do nothing about it.

Leads opened and closed in front of us, the floes banged into each other, sometimes they actually slipped and slid on top of each other. We just walked on and on, coming to more water, turning round, trying another way, going along the edges of ridges which had water the other side. There were some very soft crossings, and when Matty said 'move', you moved very fast. You felt so unsafe, and when crossing small cracks in the ice, which before you had not thought about, now you were thinking 'what if it moves!'. I do not think that until the day before we had realised just how fast the ice could move and split apart and come together.

We then came over a ridge at the end of a lead. Denise and Matty had crossed over when Victoria said: 'It's moving'. I do not think I have ever moved so fast. Paula was at the end, Denise grabbed her hand and heaved her over. Paula had said she liked being in raw nature, but did find it very scary. The ridge moved up and grew a little in height and then stopped after two minutes, but we were over by then. The noise is the worst part, it makes a kind of creaking/groaning sound. Having got to the other side we found that we were on a slightly larger island than the one we had left. We walked round it, there were a lot of islands moving around, we had more jumping over little leads, then the ice seemed to calm down a bit. Some were very small leads, some big, it was extremely frightening. We felt very helpless and very much in the hands of fate, but I think that having come through this made us all much stronger. All we could think of was whether we would manage to find a landing strip on Thursday. We set up camp on an island, but it was slightly older looking ice and the extraordinary thing was that the moment we were in the tent we felt safe. I think it was the worst day of my life - worse than being told I had breast cancer, as that is something you cannot see, but in the Arctic the reality is there in front of you and there seems no escape.

Why did falling in shake me up so much? It did not when it happened; it was the next day. I think that finding myself not in control of the situation was the scary part. Normally you can, to a certain extent, avoid nasty things, or make them less bad or whatever, but here I was, sitting on a chunk of ice two hundred miles from land, twelve hours or more from help, relying on my own resources and those of my friends. I think that this brought the team idea home.

What annoyed me was that I have always thought that I had control of things, and to find I had not bugged me. Perhaps also I have always thought of myself being quite strong mentally, and to find that this episode upset me the next day was in itself upsetting. Have I not got the strength I thought I had? Or is one still strong because one can acknowledge that one did get upset, and did not feel strong? A paradox, but interesting to analyse oneself. Perhaps its a good thing for one's character to be knocked down, go through how you feel and then you can get going again with the changed you. I do not know! All very deep and meaningful!

*

Victoria:

Lying in bed last night I had serious nightmares. What if the pulk had gone down and Mum/Me/Denise had not got our harness off? Also, what if I had gone under, tried to come up and found the ice was solid. Reality certainly hit in and I did not sleep at all well. Imagine if I had lost Mum - it really does not bear thinking about. There we were respecting the Arctic, but it is so unpredictable. When the ice is under pressure it goes solid, but the moment there is no pressure it just becomes water/slush. Quite incredible. You do think that you will die within seconds of being in the water, but your adrenalin and body warmth keep you going for some time.

It really was a day from hell, I hated every second and had a really grotty time. I had the wobbles by the evening, having thought that I was all right yesterday. We spent the whole day hopping from one island/frozen lump to another. The ice was moving all the time, and speed was of the essence. Everything just kept on moving right in front of our eyes. It was as if we had been cocky about the environment that we were in, and this was Mother Nature putting us in our place. At one stage I was going over a ridge and it started cracking and groaning under me. I shouted to move, and suddenly it rose up and Paula only just got across. Other bits were spectacular, but all you could see was this sea of water (with currents like a river) and big islands and small islands. It seemed endless and probably was!

A big worry for all of us was crossing leads. What would happen if it opened up when we were on it? How would we get across? However we could not spend the next week or so not crossing any lead we came to, as we would make no progress whatsoever. The only way to approach the problem was to be philosophical and take a calculated risk i.e. we would take all necessary precautions and the rest was in the hands of fate. I was getting totally fed up and very emotional every time that Paula said how wonderful it was to see raw nature. I eventually screamed at her and once she got stuck on the moving pressure ridge she soon stopped talking about the virtues of a dangerous environment. It was the unpredictability and helplessness of the situation that scared me; we were literally in the hands of the gods. I truly believe it was a miracle from God when the ice moved together.

I just did not like having no control. I did not mind some risk, but this seemed too much. I really had had enough and it was taking all my courage to keep going. When I went all wobbly the team was great. I wished I could have been strong, and held my emotions in check - but just thinking about what could have happened to Mum gave me a horrible bottomless pit feeling in my stomach. I wondered just how long that feeling would stay with me - or if I would ever lose it.

Chapter Eight

DIARIES: Find Your Own Runway

Wednesday 23rd April

Sue:

We had now drifted through two time zones, from Resolute to Ontario to New Brunswick, so for calculations there was a two hour time difference in the sun. A few more weeks and we would be on GMT! One of the oddest things was to be walking and not need a map, though one might have been useful sometimes. Our drift was three miles east - it was as if the east had a magnet drawing us there each night.

I got up feeling really scared and worried. Before the swim, when I was still in bed, I was warm and secure. But now I woke up feeling worried sick. Not despair, but just wondering how would we get out of this area of ice, and where do we go from here? When we went out of the tent first thing, we saw that the huge lump of ice we had crossed the night before was now separated from us by another pressure ridge, and our island had halved in size. So we were on an ever decreasing island.

After breakfast we found a crossing It was rather soft ice, but manageable. The worry was that things were still moving, but we all whizzed across, then crossed one or two more leads, but the chunks of ice were getting more and more frozen. By the time the first hour was up we were on several flat pans: relief.

We then came to a huge field of rubble, luckily well frozen. Before Monday we would have gone through without a second thought, but now there was the initial worry that it might suddenly start moving. It did not, and by the time we had got to the other side everyone felt fine. It looked well established and there was a little dusting of snow, though there were one or two dampish looking patches. The thought in the back of our minds was that if it did start moving we would be in deeper trouble than the swimming day.

We got to the other side, and wonder of wonders, a snow pan, one more ridge and rubble - and we were away, six miles in total. We had come to a very flat area, hardly any ridges and a real confidence inspiring day, apart from the first hour or so. Denise admitted she had been very nervous the day before too, with all the moving leads, but by now we were all in a very cheerful frame of mind, having clocked up a reasonable mileage. We climbed onto a huge lump of ice to see if we could see any leads or flat pans, but as we were virtually at sea level the horizon is always so near that visibility is limited.

Monday's episode gave us all quite a severe shock, and made us realise that the Arctic is a fearsome place. Before then we had crossed leads and climbed ridges without seriously considering that they could move or open up. Seeing those huge rivers of rubble moving along, shifting vast icebergs, lumps of ice floes, made one feel that this was similar to the creation - but thank heavens we had no more of that apart from the first few minutes when we left our island. Seeing ridges rise up in front of you making their primeval creaking is one of the most awe-inspiring but terrifying things you can experience. In retrospect the first easy week had made us complacent.

We were going to have to start looking for a landing strip. My one worry was that we might find more open leads, but Matty and Denise thought not. Perhaps they were just being optimistic, but I doubted it, as the seascape/ice scape had developed into a series of flat open pans, and we saw only one very small lead.

My lasting impressions of tent life: Matty and Denise strip washing themselves, then, trousers still down, drying themselves over the stoves, a bit whiffy, Victoria said, when you are sitting next to one of them, and cooking the supper at the same time! But better that, and nearly clean than really smelly. None of us did get very disgusting, apart from the odd bit of splash back, which you can pick off when it freezes, which takes no more than a minute or two. Matty woke us up every morning with her 'rise and shine'; luckily I was always awake just before so it was not so bad. The temperature inside the tent was always warm once we had lit the stoves and the sun shone through, whatever the time of day. Sometimes the tent flapped in the wind, but usually quite gently. Everyone looked bleary in the morning, but got up very quickly.

Everyone had a routine. For me, it was out of bed, on with my suit, which had been a pillow during the night. I dragged my socks out of the condom and onto my feet, then covered these with bags from the Arctic Co-op in Resolute, or Sainsburys bags which had come out with me. Next on with my boots - they had usually frozen a little; it was important to do them up at night as it stopped the ice dropping into them.

After this I took the rest of my clothes out of the condom, and put them into a stuff sack. The last thing to do was to roll up my sleeping bag, having taken the water bottles out of it and handed them to the water boiler. Next you had to brush down the tent, removing the ice that had formed from people's breath during the night, then a struggle through the door, and outside to pee. Inside, meanwhile, the fires would have been lit, so when you came back in all was warm, and you could hang up your bits and pieces to dry on the line, then the first and best cuppa.

*

Victoria:

The day started off quite badly. We spent the first two or three hours going though the rubble on lead after lead. It was very scary but as there was no sign of any squidgyness whatsoever, I gradually got my confidence back. It then opened up into pan after pan with mini ridges in between and we covered a fair bit of distance. The weather was mixed, it started off cloudy and then became nice for a couple of hours. Once on the pans the wind got up and we had almost no visibility and pretty biting winds, but there were no complaints at all because it was a significant improvement on the last forty eight hours. We started to keep an eye open for landing strips, at least us four did, and we hoped to have it confirmed on the radio that changeover would definitely be Friday.

I could not understand why my bottom had had tingling feelings in it for the last few days. I finally discovered the answer by looking at my reflection in a saucepan lid - chilblains. They were so itchy and must have come as a result of my swim in the Arctic Ocean. Other than that there were no problems at all, my back was in perfect condition, amazing considering it had played up for the last ten years of my life. I could not believe that this time next week I would be on the plane home. Despite all the scary moments I was loving it and could never describe it properly to anyone. It was just wonderful that I could share the experience with Mum.

*

Internet report

McVitie's Penguin Polar Relay - Update 23 April 1997. More

reports:

Penguin Charlie are all well but frustrated by difficult ice conditions. It would appear that the storms of the recent past have caused many breaks in the pack ice, creating a multiplicity of leads which are to say the least a nightmare to navigate through. It is like being in a maze with an uneven surface, burdened with a weight at ones feet, unable to find any high ground and with a mist around the water, restricting visibility. Furthermore the easterly drift that the team was experiencing during the storms has not abated. Consequently Penguin Charlie have to progress in a north west direction to avoid being pushed too far East. So, with a combination of a maze of leads and a drift forcing a course away from true North, despite 9 hours of walking today it was only possible to cover 5.5 miles in a northerly direction. Tonight's camp is at 86 degrees 18 mins N, 66 degrees 1 min W.

It was good to hear the team this evening on the radio, grateful messages were passed on, which I'm sure will encourage them over the last couple of days before the changeover to Penguin Delta. There are some 14 miles to go before the half way point between land and the Pole, so I am sure that this milestone will be firmly set in their minds.

It is always good to hear from the "Penguin Girls" on the radio and there is always a moment when we at base camp try to recognise the voice which is invariably distorted over the radio. I suppose using a HF radio for the first time is a bit like the first time on a telephone, some are like a duck to water whilst others are a bit more wary. It was interesting to note that Victoria Riches was a complete natural, utilizing her person to person skills that are essential in her work at Angela Mortimer Recruitment Consultants.

175

This evening Penguin Delta were listening in to the radio communications and wished their colleagues a good last couple of days . Delta have now finished their training, which has seen them in a range from practically the worst the Arctic can offer to the best. After the blizzards we have now just experienced two glorious days, big blue skies, precious little wind and a balmy 8 degrees C (minus of course).

Over the next day or so Penguin Delta will make their final preparations, check their gear time and time again (there is no going back once you are on the aeroplane) pack their pulks, weigh them in at the air carrier and then focus, each in their own individual way, on the coming days. It is a difficult time for them, there is nothing more they can do. Everyone is exceptionally fit and has trained and understands the issues of dealing with the intense cold of polar travel. We know that every member of the team is capable of handling the task ahead and in themselves as individuals they probably know they can go out and do it.

The real pressure comes from the relay element, it comes from the fact that this is not about any one individual, this is about a team of twenty whose individual strengths will enable four British women, with no polar experience, to reach the North Pole. This is where the real pressure comes from. Twelve team members have gone before and all exerted themselves hour upon hour, day upon day and have achieved. They now must do likewise and hand on that baton to the last four to give the Relay the chance of reaching the Pole.

Penguin Delta's plane won't be alone in heading North. As the light at the North Pole has become stronger over the last couple of weeks, so it has brought up here those expeditions which are travelling just that last degree or two to reach the Pole, as well as those who are simply

Saying good bye - Edward, Victoria, Jeremy, Sue, Philip.

Playing in Resolute Bay

Team Charlie ready for the off

Crossing our
first lead.

A typical arctic
day.

The intrepid du

An Ice Bridge.

A frozen lead.

Ice stalactites.

Morning!

Night!

How to occupy a storm day.

Mmmm... Food!

Sue on her island, bootless, after falling in.

The ice begins to move together!

The next day - ice melting, water everywhere!

The Arctic Loo - First. undo crap flap, check wind direction,

Next, squat and perform,

No Andrex, just snow wedges!

Hair by Riches. Denise attempting to wash her hair!

Skiis on or off,
a difficult decision.

storm getting up.
hotograph by Lynne
arke)

Crossing rubber
ice

Sue preparing the runway.

The best sight in the world! (Photograph by Lynne Clarke)

Tea with Tony

taking a plane there for that ultimate experience. Yesterday an American team set off with dogs to cover the last 120 miles from 88 degrees to the Pole. Before they set off they dropped in to our Base Camp to see how the Penguin Relay was doing.

What astounded me was that they said as far as they were aware everyone in America seemed to know about the British women's relay to the Pole. Apparently it is covered regularly on prime national television, CNN etc. and was carried recently from the east coast to the west coast on the *Today* TV show. Equally, here in Canada we see regular coverage updating Canadians on the progress of this unique event. Yet in Britain the TV companies seem to think the public wouldn't be interested in this British event although the USA, NZ, Canada and others are. It beats me but then again I'm not a British media man!

193 miles gone, 207 to go. **End**

*

Thursday 24th April

Sue:

We left the camp feeling cheerful, but our day took a downturn after about an hour, as when we were having a drink a small pressure ridge beside us suddenly started moving. We looked across and saw a huge chunk of sheet ice moving, totally silently, which made it somehow more menacing. It then ground to a halt, so we very quickly crossed the pressure ridge that had moved, and then the bit where the ice island had collided with ours. But who was actually moving, us, or it? You do not know in the Arctic, you cannot tell, it is full of optical illusions. It is a world that does not really exist. You think of the ice fields as land, but that is an illusion, it can break, or grow at any time, beneath your feet, in front of you. Nothing is what your mind thinks it is. Your mind is programmed for land, and so it relates everything it sees to land. You have to retrain yourself and your mind to accept a new world.

We had quite a lot of open water again, and miles and miles of pressure ridges. We just hoped Delta would be able to come the next day. We had all had a marvellous time, but by now everyone felt they would like to get home. We found a landing strip five hundred yards long - it was multi-year ice and did not seem too bad. It was probably the only flat ice for miles. We found it about 2.00pm, but decided not to walk on looking for another one, this would do.

The weather now seemed to be changing. I thought to myself that perhaps we should have stopped by last night's camp site, I felt I should not be down, but by now I realised that I would like to get home, and if we moved I could not see any better chance of finding another landing strip. It was an Alice in Wonderland world. Nothing was what it seemed, you did not know what you were coming to as you had no map, or what was behind you, because it would all have changed.

✦

Victoria:

We walked for six hours but only covered two more miles, as we had slipped back south overnight and most of the day was spent making up lost ground. This gave us a grand total of 68 miles North and 33.5 miles East. Whoops! Matty said that we had actually walked further than Bravo if we count the true miles, also if we worked in real miles rather than nautical it was a hundred, which sounded better. We set off in good spirits with a lovely sunny day and climbed a few ridges and had some pans but then hit lead country. I started to lose some of my confidence and had to use all my self control not to always make Paula and Lynne go first. I was convinced that changing our walking order on the 'swimming' day had been a bad omen, very superstitious of me.

Immediately after one break we were standing up and preparing to go over a ridge when it started rumbling and moving. What was it with this ice? I would be glad to get off, it was like walking on jelly. We began to wonder if we would ever find a runway as everywhere we looked there were leads or moving bits of rubble. I decided to say a prayer, and sure enough we soon came to a perfect spot, and after pacing it etc. we radioed in to 263 (Resolute Bay). They told us they were unlikely to have a plane until tomorrow, but it was worth a try. We were therefore staying put until resupply. Was this another act of God? All we needed now was good weather. The runway must be half a mile long and a quarter of a mile wide with all the bumps facing in the same direction. It would be sad to leave the ice as we had had some pretty good times but it would be such a relief to be on dry land.

Mum was in a totally dizzy mood, she is known as 'Dizzy Dora'. While she may be the most organised and efficient person in day to day life, she is useless in a confined space. Everything was kept in a plastic bag and she regularly lost her bits, only to rediscover them shortly after! Never go camping with Mum. Spirits were high in the tent, Matty did her washing (socks, gloves etc.), and Denise even washed her hair, aided by Mum. There is a theory that the longer you leave your hair without putting shampoo on it, the more it naturally cleans itself. This it totally untrue, my hair was horrible after one month of not being washed and

Denise's was disgusting after nearly two months on the ice. We were so convinced that we were going to be picked up off the ice that Paula even cut off her Tilly knickers with a pair of penknife scissors and then proceeded to bury them.

*

Friday 25th April
Sue:

We were woken up by Matty's rise and shine at 6.45 am and radioed in to Resolute - 263 - but were told that they could not send an aeroplane as the weather was closing in. We decided to walk and make a bit more distance north, looking for another runway at the same time. While we ate our breakfast though, the weather worsened, and blizzard conditions made it impossible to go out. We spent the day in the tent chatting and playing cards. Victoria and I played Malice and Spite for hours, and we all played charades which was all rather bizarre. Then we sang songs from musicals and guessed them, quite an enjoyable afternoon! We were still slipping east, which was rather worrying. In the late afternoon the sky started clearing, we all hoped it would be better the next day and there would be the resupply and changeover.

*

Victoria:

When we called Resolute the weather reports were bad. It looked good with us, but sure enough it soon clouded over. Having been told that we were off and having to look for another runway, not what we wanted, Denise and Matty suddenly said to stay put, as we had no chance

180

of finding a runway in those weather conditions (the relief on our faces!)
So we entertained ourselves by playing charades, cards, reading and
updating our diaries.

*

Internet report

McVitie's Penguin Polar Relay - Update 25 April 1997. More
reports:

Weather delays are hitting the changeover between Charlie and
Delta. **End**

*

Saturday 26th April

Sue:

Resolute now said they would not come to this landing strip, it
was not suitable; I think that Denise got fussed on the radio and did not
give the right description. It was multi-year ice with some sastrugi, but
not too bad and quite long, but it did have some quite large pressure
ridges one end. So we got up at 6.30 am and left at 9.00am. Paula was
sick in the night - she was feeling awful, so after a while we took all the
stuff out of her pulk, put it into mine and Lynne's, and Victoria then
attached the pulk to hers, it was not too hard. We had a few leads to begin
with, then rubble, then an appalling mountain of rubble/pressure ridge.
It took an hour to get across, we then came to two large open pans, but it
was much too bumpy for a landing strip.

The sun appeared which made it easier to see if there was a
likelihood of finding anything suitable. I think we were all beginning to

worry about what would happen - we had food and fuel till Monday, but then what? I felt much more fatalistic now. I think that once Friday, the projected changeover day, had passed it somehow became different. Matty said there was a lot of emotion around at changeover time. It was very difficult for them too. My tea bags had nearly run out, I had hardly any left, by now they had to do about six cups of tea, and I froze them in between brews.

We came across some leads - frozen - and walked across them, hoping to set up camp, as it appeared to be not such new ice, quite safe. It was very misty again because of all the open water, and the clouds seemed very leaden, almost as if they were full of snow. It was a very flat light. The sun had virtually disappeared. Everyone was rather upset in the morning, it seemed it would be another never-ending day looking for a landing strip. We camped on the edge of the lead, which overnight bumped into the ice floe opposite. The strange thing is that you were never aware of this happening when in your tent, we seemed to drift so gently that the impact of ice floes on each other is never felt. I hoped that we would be able to leave this lead country, I did so HATE leads, and wished I did not feel nervous crossing them. I did find them incredibly scary, particularly after the day when the whole world seemed to be on the move. We all hoped that the elusive landing strip would turn up within the next twenty four hours.

I think that each team did get psyched up for the changeover, knowing that they would be walking for two and a half weeks. By now we were looking forward to seeing our families again, so when an unexpected delay arose it was nerve wracking for everyone. Poor Lynne did worry about seeing her boys, and I think seeing her sit there, looking

182

at their pictures and getting more and more upset, did actually affect and upset us all. The sun tried to come out, and at one stage we did have real sunshine - it gave a great mental boost to have real light. The flat light we had been having somehow makes you feel rather flat. As the light changed, so did our feelings.

*

Victoria:

Surprise, surprise another day on the ice. The pilots decided they did not like the sound of our runway so we had to move. We four felt that Denise got in a fluster when describing it, so the pilots got confused and therefore rejected it, very annoying. So off we went, poor Paula had been sick overnight so I took her pulk and some bits and bobs and the rest was divided out. We walked for nine and a half hours and during this time we crossed the Alps, came across short and smooth or long and bumpy runways, helicopter pads i.e. everything but a suitable airstrip. It was decidedly unfunny as we were going to run out of food on Monday. I had also realised that if we did not get the flight back home on Tuesday (the plane only goes twice a week), I would miss the wedding of Veryan, one of my oldest friends.

My spirits were pretty high though, as I had become philosophical. Lynne was fairly low and Paula was not too good. Mum had a major wobbly when crossing a lead, and also when I led two pulks over a crack and they fell "in the water you stupid child!" There was no water in sight as it was all frozen, but I think Mum was having a very bad day. Talked to Resolute and there was a plane on standby. We were determined to find a runway the next day. I felt fine after nine and a half hours of walking, my body was raring to go. Having said that, I was

183

getting worried about catching the plane and would be seriously annoyed if I missed Veryan's wedding, but I realised that I would be very lucky if I did make it. Everyone's spirits were pretty low and we were conscious that we had to find an airstrip because the next day was cutting it too fine re food etc.

*

Internet report

McVitie's Penguin Polar Relay - Update 26 April 1997. More reports:

Penguin Charlie's position as at tonight is 86degrees14 minutes North, 62 degrees23 minutes West. That's strange, you may say, I thought they were at 86deg18N, 66deg1W two days ago? Your memory serves you well. The last two days is a good reminder that this is not just a "walk in the park" and that, unlike the Antarctic, this is not ice capped land but is a constantly moving ice pack.

Yesterday, Penguin Charlie walked for some 6 hours in pretty inclement weather, in particular a strong penetrating wind from which it is important to keep your face protected. At the end of the day's slog they checked their GPS reading only to find that they were still at the same position north as when they started, 86deg18mins. Furthermore their "westerly" position had moved a little east despite the team travelling in a north west direction throughout the day. This level of drift is playing havoc with all the expeditions on the ice and daily presents the question of whether to proceed true north or to compensate by walking partially into the drift.

Today the weather deteriorated even further making any travel very difficult, so bearing in mind that they were camped near what appeared to be an acceptable airstrip, they stayed put but inevitably ended up drifting south east during the course of the day.

This evening, following a radio conversation between Penguin Charlie and the air pilots it was agreed that in view of the weather, their chosen airstrip was probably inappropriate, therefore it was decided to head north and seek an alternative strip later today.

Good morning ..... (Penguin Sue, Reserve here). It's now morning on 26/4/97, we have spoken to Penguin Charlie who are at this moment setting off to clock up as many miles as they can, and find a suitable airstrip. Meanwhile, Penguin Delta remain on standby, itching to get on with the job they are here to do. They are like racehorses at the starting gate, very restless. Spending their time packing and re packing, writing diaries, letters to loved ones, listening to music, eating, going out for walks and skiing.

Yesterday, four of us on skis set off to ski back down to the hamlet across the bottom of the runway, up on to the hills overlooking the airport. Blue sky, bright sunlight, the temp. was -15 c and a cold wind was starting to pick up from the north causing snow to blow snakelike around our feet and off into the wilderness. There wasn't a lot of chit chat, the girls were quietly thinking to themselves. Just wanting to get some exercise rather than sit in No. 75, the house we are staying in down at the Hamlet. It took us about two hours over the snow and ice covered hills, following the strange Inuit cairns which are perched on the top of each high point.

It's a real joy to be out on skis without pulling a pulk behind you, and we had a few laughs when we kept tumbling over trying to do ski tricks, which are very hard on cross-country skis with skins on. At

185

one point our speed doubled, when Juliette thought she'd found some polar bear tracks! Rosie also pulled out a mirror, and we had a little signalling practice using the sun's reflection, just in case we had to dazzle a charging polar bear!

The changeover was to have taken place yesterday, but bad weather up on the ice (very windy) postponed this, also the pilot was not happy with the airstrip Penguin Charlie had found. There were BIG discussions on the radio last night with regard to the length and condition of the airstrip. The outcome of this being a no go, because of the presence of a 12' pressure ridge close to one end. So Charlie will radio in usual time tonight, hopefully with good news and the change over will take place as soon as a plane can reach them.

About my stay here in Resolute Bay. Well, I don't know quite where to start! I've probably seen more of the place than anyone. I've had more free time to explore and get to know the locals. It has not been easy for me being reserve, but very frustrating, knowing I could do it. Not really fitting into any team, but training just as hard if not harder than many relay members, just in case my services are called on. I keep telling myself, on the positive side, that I've done my best and if I was ever needed I'm here and I'm ready. Maybe I've earned my place on the next expedition.

I've trained out here with Charlie and helped train Delta, and I've got to know the girls and admire each and every one for their determination to give it their best. I'm sure like me, they've each been to the North Pole and back many times in their dreams. Also, a big, big well done to the teams that have completed their legs and to the teams waiting to go, I hope they all get out there, give it their very best and enjoy

186

themselves.

> This is Sue Self signing out from Resolute Bay.
>
> 189 miles gone, 211 miles to go **End**

*

Sunday 27th April

Sue:

It was a day of appalling light, completely flat, and looking for a runway was well nigh impossible. When we left the tent we immediately had to cross a lead at the end of a ridge. Denise went on ahead to see if she could find a way out of this area of leads, though not too far ahead, as since the dunking we all like to be much closer together than we were in the first week. You realise that you do need a team member near enough to effect a rescue if necessary.

We came to a vast area of huge snow chunks which took us several hours to get through. Should we take our skis off and perhaps fall in the holes, or risk breaking them? There was no way we could see what the ice was like when we got to the other side, so we stopped and put the tent up to wait for better weather. Matty and Denise wanted to make some miles and there was this sort of conflict of interest, Paula was not strong now, and was getting slower, her sickness had taken it out of her. We thought that if we stayed in this area we would perhaps be able to find the elusive runway when the weather lifted.

We talked to Resolute, who said if we ran out of food and fuel they would do a drop. We did feel sorry for Penguin Delta, they must have been very worried and the waiting must have been very difficult, as you cannot go and do anything in case you get the call to the plane. Lynne was very worried and upset, thinking about her boys, but you had to accept it, there was nothing you could do.

Morale between Victoria and myself was very good but Lynne and Paula were down, and were walking quite slowly. Because I knew that we would not starve I felt I could go on a lot more and walk further. We received messages over the radio for Matty about pitta bread. Rick of Northwest Passage, (another expedition) had heard on the radio that she wanted bread. His, having been left behind on his resupply, was at Resolute so he arranged that his base camp team would send it to Matty at the changeover. Everyone listens to each other's radio messages and nothing is private. The pilots said it was like a soap opera!

*

Victoria:

We skied for five and a half hours and spent ages testing various pans, but there was such appalling light we could not tell if it was suitable unless we tested each one individually, which was wasteful. So we set up camp on a vaguely possible strip, I did not want to raise my hopes, and waited for the weather to clear. Having spoken to Mike on the radio it seemed that the weather would be great in the evening and all the next day. He also told us not to panic as they would, if necessary, drop emergency fuel and food. My initial feeling was 'forget that, we want out'. In reality though I was becoming more philosophical, and having got my confidence back was enjoying it again. We knew that we could not do anything and I had resigned myself to the fact that I would not make Veryan's wedding, so it was not so bad.

Morale was not great though as Matty and Denise wanted to

188

make miles and all we wanted to do was go home, very tricky. Mike had to chat up Delta to see how flexible they would be re staying on the ice because they were not going to get very long at this rate. I began to wonder what would happen to Penguin Echo. They were supposed to leave the UK the next day, would they be delayed by a few days?

*

Internet report

McVitie's Penguin Polar Relay - 27th April 1997. More reports:

Hello from the members of Penguin Delta - Sarah, Juliette, Andre and Rosie.

We are going through a difficult time here at the moment. Waiting to get on the ice, but first being stopped by bad weather and now by the lack of a suitable landing strip. We all are trying to cope with the wait in our own way and it's interesting to note how different that is for each of us, but it's fair to say that the overall atmosphere is more subdued. With our training completed, we still make a point of going out, between radio communications, for several hours a day both to keep acclimatised and to help keep our spirits up.

It cannot be easy for Penguin Charlie either. Currently battling against a strong south easterly drift, their quest to find a suitable landing strip continues, whilst trying to maintain a good daily mileage.

At every moment we await our 'scramble' call., We are always prepared to go at a minutes notice; packed and eating as if it were our last non-dehydrated meal!

Tonight Penguin Charlie are camped at 86degs21minsN 61degs22minsW having covered three nautical miles today in poor conditions. The mileage as ever is important but at this precise time is secondary to trying to find a suitable airstrip. With the weather forecast being for improving conditions overnight, Charlie set up camp at 15.00 local time this afternoon (Sunday) in order to get some rest before trying to do some further mileage overnight in conditions hopefully better suited to finding a strip.

Inevitably preparations for an airdrop of extra food and fuel to Penguin Charlie are being made, just in case the changeover cannot be made within the next day or so. Fingers crossed, such measures won't be needed.

196 miles gone, 219 to go. The halfway point still proves elusive.
End

Chapter Nine

Happy Landings & Sad Partings

Monday 28th April

Sue:

Was this going to be the day? We were up at 2.00am. You could almost see the sun, there was a little snow coming down, and still very flat light. We were not too sure about the flat pan by the campsite, it seemed a little short, so we went off exploring, leaving our pulks by the tent, trying to find landing strips. We criss-crossed a few mini leads, but nothing suitable in that direction. When we all got back to the camp site we decided that the original pan was the best, so we measured it. It was perhaps a little short, but it looked as if it might do. Denise radioed in to base camp, and they said the plane would be with us in about twelve to fourteen hours, plus the extra rations just in case they could not land. So we started marking and moving snow to make the runway smoother - I still would not believe that we were going away until the plane took off with us on board.

It was an odd sort of day. Matty and Denise were in a strange mood, another day wasted not skiing, it must have been quite difficult for them and extremely frustrating - a number of days had been wasted waiting for the weather to be suitable for the changeover. For all of us the unpredictability of life during our Arctic sojourn was our main concern. We were always walking into the unknown and you never knew what lay ahead. If you wanted to retrace your steps, you could not, as the ice might have broken up or drifted away. Even when waiting for the plane, the fact that it was in the air on its way meant nothing. The weather could change, the ice might not be smooth enough, or it might have split apart and prevented a landing, so even up to the last moment we could not say that we knew what was going to happen.

*

Victoria:

Got up at 2 am having done hourly shifts to check on the weather. We scouted all the pans again and sure enough there were two possibilities. After five hours of digging, shovelling and stamping we chose one. First Air decided they liked the sound of the runway, and within an hour Penguin Delta were on their way. I was so excited and relieved, but until they actually landed I would not believe it. Spirits very quickly rose and we spent the morning doing changeover details e.g. who gets skis, poles, audio and video equipment. I did not want to get excited but......

*

Sue:

The pilots did not like our runway. We could hear the plane in the distance, getting louder and louder, we all rushed out of the tent in a state of high excitement, and jumped up and down waving to Penguin Delta, whom we could see looking out of the windows; we knew just how they felt at this stage. They circled round and round and round for three quarters of an hour, and each time we waved less, jumped less, until in the end we were just standing helplessly, wondering if there was any chance of a landing. Paula lit up her last cigarette, we stood in silence, no one talking; all just wishing, praying that they would land.

We were in contact with the pilots over the radio and they said that our six hours of smoothing had not made an unsuitable runway any

192

better. The plane kept dipping down and trying runways, but just as you thought they had landed it took off again. They were about to go back as their fuel was getting low.   Eventually we saw the plane, miles away trying a strip, down twice and up again, then down - and we waited, and waited, and waited, then the roar of reversing engines. They had landed.

We stood for a few seconds hardly daring to believe it. Then wild excitement, we took a bearing and hoped we had got it right. We took the tent down in double quick time and we were off. I do not think anyone has moved as fast as us! They had landed about two miles away, and it took an hour for us to get there, it must have been the fastest mile ever done in the Arctic. When we got to the final pressure ridge we agreed that we should all go round the corner together.

It was a very emotional moment seeing the others. It was a glorious day, very sunny, much colder, all we had been praying for, but a wonderful start for Delta and a wonderful day to have as our last memory of the ice. I would never be so far North again. We helped change over all the equipment, including skis. The plane engines had to be wrapped up the whole time we were on the ice. One is kept running the whole time, except for the refuelling. Matty gave me all her correspondence and asked me to ring her husband Paul and tell him how she was. It was a very sad moment saying goodbye, particularly to Denise, with whom we had become especially close.

We took photographs of the team and handing over the penguin, our relay baton. The others seemed to be in really good order, despite the long wait. Carl and Amy, the pilots, refuelled the aeroplane, but when everyone had climbed out and the fuel cans had been removed the whole plane tipped up onto its tail. Someone had to go and stand in the front for it to get level again.

We left at about 8.30 pm. Looking down it was hard to believe that it was such hard work walking. We were sad, but relieved to be off the ice, yet the second we took off was dreadful, none of us wanted to go now. Looking down on the leads, ridges, pans and amazing variety of terrain I felt an incredible sadness. I knew I would never be there again, never see those sights again, and how lucky I had been. How few people have ever been there, seen it, experienced the colours, the sounds, the lack of smell, the fear, the sheer enjoyment and thrill when you feel that you really will burst with happiness. I definitely felt a lot closer to God and my faith became stronger. I feel very appreciative of what I have, and what I had seen and been allowed to see. I think that we have all left something of ourselves behind - and I think that none of us will ever be the same again.

We all have a new sense of wonder now, realising the sheer power of nature. I certainly felt different, and looked down on the Arctic ice realising what we had done; not much compared to some expeditions, but we were very ordinary people, and I think that we showed others that you can have a dream - and achieve it. The strange thing was that however hostile the landscape, however frightening the events, however alien man is here, we did not feel threatened. We did not feel that the Arctic was against us, or at least more against us than anything else, considering this was not man's natural environment.

We sat in a single row of seats with the very smelly oil drums next to us. As we took off they started banging. We had been told that food had been left on the plane for us - it was shortbread! It was very noisy, there was frost on the inside of the window for the first hour, then

194

it was too warm. Ellesmere looked amazing: fjords, glaciers, the sea pushing up against the land and the ridges formed going forever into the distance. There were endless mountains, the sun still shining on them at 10.30 pm. What a landscape, but it was nice to be above the land!

It was an extremely bumpy descent down to Eureka, the wind was buffeting us quite considerably. We had a fantastic welcome there, Dave Urquhart came and picked us up, and there was a glass of home brew beer waiting for us. They then let us use the shower, wonderful, my socks smelled unbelievably disgusting, even when wrapped up in a bag! They asked if we wanted food and took us to Aladdin's cave. A fridge with fruit juice, carrots, chopped up celery, dry crackers, we really pigged out on hot buttered toast too. It was awful, we just grabbed. Then back for more beer. David Hempleman-Adams and the Rune Gjeldnes were there in the bar, they had had to be picked up, because of a badly damaged pulk (his was 340 lbs - ours 140 lbs). It had a huge hole, but the weight and length couldn't have helped when smashing down on ridges.

*

Victoria:

We were sitting in the tent waiting for the plane, having sorted out our pulks and all dressed in our thermals ready for the cold plane. Suddenly the best sound in the world. There was a steady drone and we all fought to get out of the tent door first. A comedy act! Then right above us and really low was the plane, you could see figures at the window, it was a very emotional moment for all of us. Paula even lit her last fag!

But the plane did not land and when Denise spoke to the pilot on the radio he said that the runway was too short. He circled over and over, testing numerous possible runways, for what seemed like an eternity - in reality for one hour. He then said that he was going to drop the emergency provisions. We begged him to have one more look for a runway and he then kept on testing this strip miles away.

Eventually he landed, we could hear the engines reversing thrust, so we took a bearing and then skied as fast as possible, because he could not stay on the ground for more than an hour or so. We were *soooo* hot as we had all our clothes on and were skiing very fast. I was terrified that we would not find the plane because the terrain was fairly rough and you can not see a white plane in the snow! After a while we saw the wing tips, but even then we wondered if it was a mirage, our imagination. Luckily it was the real thing. We went round the corner together and there were Penguin Delta running towards us and the plane. Amazing, so wonderful, yet so sad....

We loaded up the plane and had a very quick catch up. It was great to see them all, they all looked as nervous as we had been two weeks previously. It was a weird feeling though, as I was almost jealous of Matty and Denise, they were ours and now another team was going to have them to themselves. I did not want anyone else to share my experiences. At one stage the tail of the plane hit the ground because when loading the front was not balanced. It must have been a very funny sight as we all lifted up the tail of the plane while they sorted out the ballast. Saying goodbye to Denise and Matty was so sad; they had become such a part of our lives. It was such a safe feeling to be on the plane, the ice was not going to crack underneath me any more. Flying back we could see how much the ice had opened up in the storms. We all sat and looked at it in silence.

Poor Lynne was very ill on the plane, she was even sick. We landed at Eureka, Dave Urquhart picked us up and took us down to the weather station. He told us that Dave Hempleman-Adams and his Norwegian colleague Rune Gjeldnes were there also, because their expedition had failed due to a broken pulk, there was no way it was repairable.

We chatted to them briefly, but were more interested in the food that the weather station was offering us. We even had an attempt at a shower, and got to sit on a loo properly. I will never forget it, sitting on the loo, reading a National Geographic magazine and using real loo paper. Bliss!! The food was just wonderful, not very exciting but it was not rations. They had even made some homebrew beer for us, interesting taste.

Tuesday 29ᵗʰ April

Sue:

We discovered that Carl, our pilot, had taught skiing for a year at Glenshee in the sixties, perhaps I had seen him then! He is something of a local celebrity, having been involved in flying most expeditions on and off the ice - he seemed to have met every Arctic explorer. After eating we had staggered off to a wonderfully comfortable bunk house with sheets, shower and a loo. It was hard to go to sleep in a bed, we left our doors open so we could talk to each other! We must have been like prisoners of war, who on their return home had to sleep on the floor!

We had a wake up call at 7.00 am but we were all up. And then a marvellous breakfast of bacon, egg, sausage, eggy bread, toast, marmalade, fruit juice, Earl Grey tea. Everything that we had dreamed of on the ice. They were so kind at Eureka, and it meant so much to us to be offered the comfort. One of the First Air pilots said he was amazed at how well we all looked when we come back off the ice - no sunburn, frostbite, frostnip or scabby bits. We had taken care of our skins every day and felt better for it.

David Hempleman-Adams was on our flight back to Resolute with his damaged pulks. Apparently they put up both the British and Norwegian flag each night, and said God save the Queen and God save the King.

When we took off we could see that the ice was beginning to break up. There were patches of open water, an incredible vivid blue. The snow would start to go in two weeks, then all the flowers would appear, hence Eureka is known as the 'Garden spot of the Arctic'. You could see the ice cracking on the lakes, and they were almost blue as well. There were vast glaciers going down to the sea, a lot of Ellesmere is covered by glaciers.

By this stage there were only five teams left on the ice: Northwest Passage, Kono, Polar Free, Dutch and the McVitie's Penguin Polar Relay.

We arrived back at Resolute. Champagne on the runway, in a very cold wind. It had started to freeze, slushy champagne is quite difficult to drink, especially out of the bottle. It was a terrible rush: we arrived at about midday and only had six hours to be debriefed, change, shower, pack and catch our aeroplane. So we paid a quick visit to the Rookery, where they told us the Queen and the Queen Mother had sent messages to Penguin Delta via Rosie's mother, which was very good to hear.

It was then down to No. 75 to sort out our clothes. Diane took us from the Rookery down to the hamlet, a blizzard was blowing and we did a complete spin in the snow and ended up by the airport sign facing the way we came! Luckily someone coming went and called Gary who pulled her out. Meanwhile Nobby, who had been following us, took us on to the house.

I have never packed so quickly, or so badly, trying to fit dirty Arctic gear into cases and, trying to sort out the clothing that Penguin Echo would be using when they arrived that evening This had to be washed, as they would not have liked it much otherwise! Then it was back to the Rookery and then to the airport. After the peace and steady pace of life on the ice the frenetic six hours in Resolute was very hard to come to terms with. We all felt in a sort of dreamlike state, glad to be back, but every thought was with those on the ice.

It was very sad to say goodbye to Gary and Diane. We saw Echo arrive, and then, that was it, goodbye Resolute. I wished we had had more time to unwind and get used to being back. You needed quiet thinking time to come back to the real world, it had all happened much too quickly. It was a terrible wrench to leave it all.

As we flew out we could see the sea breaking up, and we realised that spring was on the way. It was white snow the whole way North from Edmonton in March, but by now there were brown trees. Flying down to Yellowknife you could see how the land developed like the sea; pressure ridges in dead straight lines or gashes going off at angles; then suddenly there were trees, and on all the lakes there were skidoo marks, disappearing into trails in the woods. Millions of lakes, just defrosting, very flat, it went on for at least two and a half hours, a haven for midges in the summer.

There was a beautiful evening light at Yellowknife. Delicious salmon on the plane and David Hempleman Adams gave us both wine. It is extraordinary to realise that we have now become sort of 'explorers' and can talk about things to someone like David that previously would have been Greek to us. Yet another meal between Yellowknife and Edmonton, salmon and Mars bars, crackers and cheese and brandy coffee, compliments of Canadian Airlines. So there we were in Edmonton, almost at the end of our fantastic experience of a life time.

*

Victoria:

We even had real beds to sleep in, courtesy of the Eureka guys, very weird and almost uncomfortable. None of us were used to them and we talked for most of the night. The welcome we received at Eureka was just amazing, we were made to feel like heroes and were treated like royalty. I will never forget it, and it sums up the friendly attitude of all the people we met in the Arctic. Next morning we caught the plane on to Resolute, and Dave Hempleman-Adams and I got chatting. It turned out that he ran a children's camp each summer so I offered to help out on it, all good experience if I was to become a teacher.

We landed at Resolute, what bliss. We had got the pilots to radio ahead and remind Nobby to bring our bottle of champagne to the plane, courtesy of Moet & Chandon, however it was so cold that it was totally frozen! It was great to see everyone, but quite tricky with Sue Self as we did not want to sound too excited. It must have been very difficult for her, but not once did she complain. We called home to let them know that we were safe and sound. Phil answered the phone and screamed to

Dad that it was us, but he was not going to believe it until he saw us at Heathrow.

We had a brief catch up with everyone, we were in a mad panic to change, wash, and pack before catching the plane to Edmonton, but none of us could stop talking. It was great to see Geoff, he must have been so chuffed, as it was his training that enabled us to get there. The weather in Resolute was appalling, blizzard conditions, and we managed to do a 360^0 turn in the snow on the road down to No. 75. We survived the Arctic Ocean but almost kill ourselves in a car, very ironic. Just to put the icing on the cake, we found that the pickup had a flat tyre so there was a mad panic to repair it in time to catch the plane. Penguin Charlie certainly live on the edge. Off we went to the airport, but there was no time to stop and think because it was such a mad rush. As usual we were travelling with an extra fifteen odd bits of luggage. Everyone felt very clean and Mum and I managed to walk right past Dave and Rune because they looked so different without their beards.

It was wonderful to see Penguin Echo when they arrived off the plane, even if only for fifteen minutes. They all looked slightly bemused. The rest of Resolute looked stunned at these groups of girls exchanging loud and emotional greetings. It was desperately sad to say goodbye to Nobby, Mike and Geoff, they had played such an important part in our lives back at base. Passed on Lukas to Lucy, I only wished that she could have been there on our leg. It was amazing as we flew down towards Yellowknife how the ice had already opened up, and in some places there were vast expanses of water. Arrived at Le Duc and (oh bliss) we all, the Penguin girls and the Typhoo boys, sat in comfort, even Motel rooms seem comfy, drinking more champagne. We then went to eat and as the manager had heard of us he gave us drinks on the house. By this stage the alcohol was starting to take effect, not a good move when there was another twenty four hours of flying ahead of us!!

*

Internet report

McVitie's Penguin Polar Relay - 29th April 1997. More reports:

We left you two days ago with quite a tricky situation. It was becoming increasingly important to effect a changeover between Penguins Charlie and Delta, firstly because Charlie's food was running very low, and secondly Delta had finished their training and were eager to get going. The problem was a combination of poor weather and difficult ice conditions where landing strips are few and far between.

On Sunday night Penguin Charlie camped for a few hours only, just to take in a meal and sleep briefly before continuing on their search for an airstrip which had already been going on for two days. The pans of ice had either been flat but short, or long but bumpy. A radio call was taken here at base camp at 03.10am to say that they were walking North again to look for a strip. At 05.50am they came up again on the radio to say that they had found a strip which they thought would be adequate to land a Twin Otter.

Although the weather was still poor it was expected to improve, so Delta was "scrambled" once we had the all clear from the air carrier at 7.30am. Two litres of water per person have to be boiled so that the outgoing team has its own fluid for 12 hours, and can hit the ice running without having to stop for fluid. In practice it takes eight hours to reach the team on the ice after a refuelling stop at Eureka weather station, so changeover didn't take place till 18.00 and was further delayed when a very sympathetic pilot rejected Penguin Charlie's airstrip, and then spent an hour circling trying to find an alternative flat strip of ice that was long enough. The fact that it took him an hour in a plane to find an adequate area shows the difficult task that the team had to undertake on foot.

Precautions had been taken with food and fuel in the event that a landing could not take place - Delta had on board four days of supplies, ready to be dropped out of the cargo doors. This would certainly have produced a smile on Sue Riches' face as she said she was now down to her last tea bag, and it had already serviced five cups of water!

All's well that ends well, and the changeover was effected thanks to the combined skills of the two pilots Carl and Amy. The plane finally landed, albeit two miles from Charlie's position. I understand that the tent was dismantled in record time, and it took a quarter of the normal time to travel to the plane. The Penguin baton was handed over, an awful lot of very genuine hugs and tears were shared, then all too soon the plane left leaving Penguin Delta alone on the Arctic pack ice. It must be one of life's moments of realism when that plane takes off, and you know that this is it - the plane has gone, and you're on your own in the middle of a frozen ocean. We wish the Delta team, Juliette May, Sarah Jones, Rosie Stancer and Andre Chadwick good luck, good speed and good health.

Due to the time taken to complete the change-over it was not possible for the pilots to fly back to Resolute on the same shift, so an overnight stay was made in Eureka. There Penguin Charlie were given the heroines' welcome they deserved: a shower, clean sheets, and a fresh meal by the men who man the station. The guys at Eureka have been generous to us and we really appreciate it, though I'm sure they appreciate the women passing through just as much.

So, Penguin Charlie arrived back here at around noon and had a very quick turnaround to catch their 6.30 pm flight with Canadian Airlines, which had brought in Penguin Echo, the final team. There were great scenes in the airport terminal when the two teams met briefly, and exchanged useful tips. For Echo, seeing a radiant healthy looking Charlie team must on the one hand give them confidence but on the other remind them that their job is still to come, and they have to put the final block in place to complete what the others have done before. Penguin Echo is made up of Caroline Hamilton, Pom Oliver, Zoe Hudson and Lucy Roberts.

Tonight Penguin Delta's ARGOS position was 86deg30 minNorth, 62deg15minWest. This is a great start, nine miles on their first day leaving 210 miles to go and 205 miles behind them. **End**

*

Wednesday 30ᵗʰ April

Sue:

On our arrival in Edmonton we went to the same Thelma and Louise motel in Le Duc, a Magnum of Moet appeared, as did Dave and Rune, and we managed to down it between us, then off to the bar. By now it was 12.30 am. We ate Tacos, wonderful, and had complementary beer from the management when they heard what we had done. Bed at three o'clock, our body clocks were going mad. I woke up in the middle of the night, worried. I thought that it was dark because it had snowed and the tent was blocked in.

Next morning we gathered up our luggage, which now included

four pulks (marginally better than salami), and on to Toronto. The whole past day or so seemed to have passed in a blur: we started early on Monday morning digging our own landing strip in a seascape of white, not knowing what was going to happen, and we now found ourselves in a colourful, noisy and smelly world with ready made runways and no worries about whether the plane could land or take off. Not many holidays can end with having to find and flatten your runway. By the time we got back home it would be fifty six hours door to door - North Pole to Pattingham.

*

Thursday, 1st May
Victoria:

I was very hung over and had not slept at all well, as I kept on waking up and wondering which way was North. Had a breakfast from heaven: eggy bread, bacon, orange juice etc. It was very strange at the airport because all these people kept on coming up to us, having read about or seen us on the news. Would it be like this in the UK? I doubted it.

We managed to get upgraded for the Edmonton-Toronto flight, wonderful, drinking Chardonnay and watching *101 Dalmatians* in pure comfort. Thirty hours ago we were sitting on the ice, it was such a contrast. But does it give a healthy glow to the Arctic, and make you forget all the bad things?

A wonderful flight from Toronto to Heathrow, we saw both sunset and sunrise, the first in six weeks. The first bit of really green land we saw was the Western Isles of Scotland, then down Britain on a beautifully clear day, perfect for flying. The strange thing was that even though this was Britain it looked so similar to the Arctic, with all the fields (pans) and hedges (ridges), the only difference being that one was a white landscape and the other green.

As we approached Heathrow I began to get more excited about going home and to seeing Dad, the boys and Tessa the dog. We caused quite a stir in Heathrow with all our luggage, we looked like real explorers. Dad was mega relieved to see us, but in a real state as he was convinced that the IRA were going to blow up Heathrow while we were there.

Phil and Dad wanted to know all about everything, but I just wanted to be quiet and think about it all, the culture shock was almost too much. Had a wonderful time at Sainsburys, buying excessive amounts of fresh fruit. The colour green was so lush and the sound of wind in the trees was so wonderful, I did not realise how much I had missed it. The house looked like an Interflora shop, and the funny thing was that everyone had sent us white flowers. My sense of smell also became more acute, the smell was just amazing. The clouds are so different, you do not get fluffy types of cloud in the Arctic, it tends to be lines or streaks. Baths and showers were not nearly as exciting as I had expected. I did manage to get sunburned within one day of arriving back in England - there was a heatwave, so we had experienced a $30/40^0$ temperature rise in twenty four hours.

*

Sue:

The flight from Toronto to London seemed on one hand to take forever, yet was not really long enough to realise that for us the Arctic was in the past. I longed to get back to Jeremy, Philip, Edward and all our friends and relations, but was still terribly sad to be leaving all our friends in the North. However, we eventually landed, and of course our luggage was just about the last off, we made our way through customs, and there were Jeremy and Philip - totally unchanged, while I felt that we were totally different. Despite having not slept very well on the plane, neither of us could stop talking and trying to explain the whole feel of the expedition. Jeremy was I think, extremely glad to see us in one piece, as after the swim, Nobby had rung him up, chatted for some time, then said 'don't worry - but ...'. The moment someone says that on the telephone you immediately start worrying like mad. So there we were, in one piece, no parts having dropped off through frostbite and thrilled to be together again.

Returning in time for the General Election I felt totally disinterested, as I had missed the run up to it. We had non stop interviews, and in between them went to Sainsburys and bought huge quantities of fruit. We lay on the lawn, dozed and ate the fruit as our senses were overpowered by smells, sounds, birds, dogs and colours. Jeremy and Philip cooked us a wonderfully simple supper, asparagus, smoked salmon and beef.

We were very relieved to be home, but already we were missing the Arctic. I found it nearly impossible to think of anything else. Having been so focussed on one sole object, suddenly to have to fill your brain with other things was very difficult. Multi-tasking, something I have always been able to do, became impossible. I used to be able to do countless things at once *and* talk on the telephone! It was wonderful doing something as simple as sitting in the garden just looking around at these incredible colours. The clouds looked so different, we lost our feeling of being something tiny in an immense area. Our horizon, from being apparently limitless, had suddenly shrunk to the bounds of a hedge or a row of trees. In the Arctic vanishing point had been infinity, it had now become more accessible and was within theoretical reach.

The whole experience for me had been something totally out of my normal existence. I had never travelled rough before, so it was certainly an eye opener. But conversely, I think that perhaps I changed less than anyone else because my change had started in hospital two years before. It was very difficult to adjust to the everyday life at home, particularly in bed at night. The first few nights were very disturbed as I thought I was still on the ice. One night I saw the outline of a tree and thought it was a giant iceberg. Some nights I woke up imagining that we were moving and (the final straw), I woke up puzzled to find Jeremy in the space next to me - when we were in the tent there was no one on my right hand side. After that things returned to normal, much to his relief.

It was still very difficult not to tell people about our dunking. We had been told by Pen that if the Press wrote about it, however good a story it might be, the relatives of those still on the ice would be worried and upset. I did tell some friends as I felt it was better to talk about it. I think that not having a full debriefing, and two days to unwind at Resolute, caused a problem for Penguin Charlie. Much as we wanted to get home, a few days coming to earth and getting back to normal would have helped us when we arrived back.

*

Victoria:

I already missed the Arctic and I just wanted to be on my own. I

208

felt so empty and lonely and did not really know if I was coming or going. It was almost as if I was watching myself giving all the interviews to the press. I wanted to talk to someone who understood what we had done. Not Mum, as we had spent the last two months together, but someone who understands the Arctic, someone who I can relate to. I realised I definitely wanted to do it again, I could have easily carried more and gone on for longer. Once I got my confidence back I was fine. The power and magnitude of nature was so wonderful, and the achieving of the slightly unachievable so addictive, that I knew I had the bug. I was dreading handing in my notice the following week, a real jolt back to reality.

In the evening we went and voted, but without much interest, which was unusual for someone who read Politics at university. The best news though was that while we were away I had won £132 on the National Lottery!

But amidst the withdrawal symtoms, the pleasures and the small sadnesses, Penguin Echo were never far from our thoughts. Would they reach the Pole, or (horrible thought) in that unforgiving environment, would the precious time lost by Penguin Charlie turn out to have cost them their chance?

Chapter Ten

The Pole and After

Victoria:

Life was an anticlimax. Having spent our first few days in the UK in some sort of a dream world, I came back down to earth with a bump and had to return to my job and life in London. I was expected to carry on as before, except that nothing would be the same, I now had a totally different outlook on life. In some ways I was totally laid back. A friend of mine, Jane, drove into my car, but I was not remotely concerned and the dent is still there today. Even sitting in traffic jams or commuting on the tube did not worry me as I went into my own little dream world. However, I started to get very irritated when people made mountains out of mole hills, what was the point? Office politics suddenly started to drive me up the wall and I lost the desire to make money and always work towards targets. I had almost become gentler, less interested in material results, more concerned about making the most of the moment.

It was during this first month back in England that I made the first of two monumental decisions. I decided that I really was going to leave London and finally pursue a career that I had thought about for some time: teaching. When I broached the idea to various friends and relatives I had nothing but support and of course the odd comment - you will make a perfect teacher as you are so bossy! Telling my company, Angela Mortimer plc, was not so easy as they had been one of the expedition sponsors and I obviously felt rather guilty, them having invested so much time and money in the one thing that ultimately made me give up my recruitment career. Having got over his initial disappointment and obvious annoyance, John Mortimer was very supportive, which certainly made the transition much easier for me. In retrospect I know that my mind was definitely not on the job for the last few weeks as it became apparent that Echo were almost at the North Pole and we were about to make history.

Monday 26th May was a bank holiday, and I spent the day taking my grandfather and great aunt to visit relatives. On the way back, much to my grandfather's amusement, my mobile phone did not stop; he has always called me a yuppie! The first person to call was Ann Fleury of *The Birmingham Post*. She had always shown great interest in the expedition and it was lovely that she was the one who told me that Echo were just hours away from success. This call was followed by the BBC, various local stations and newspapers. This was it, I was so excited.

*

Sunday 25th May
Internet report

McVitie's Penguin Polar Relay - Update 25 May 1997. More reports:

If you've been a follower of this website, I don't think we need to say much other than 'the fat lady's started to sing, and she may have finished by tomorrow (Monday) night'.

Penguin Echo have stormed 16NM northwards today to reach 89 44N, 73 14W: 399 miles done; just 16 miles to go.

Matty McNair, Denise Martin, Caroline Hamilton, Pom Oliver, Zoe Hudson and Lucy Roberts are all in good shape and high spirits ...

and they are on the threshold of some remarkable achievements. The first all-women expedition to the Geographic North Pole, incorporating the first two women to have ever travelled the whole way on foot, without dogs or machines (our guides - Matty McNair and Denise Martin), and one of the largest (22 women), and most complex North Pole expeditions since the turn of the century.

Every Penguin Team - Alpha, Bravo, Charlie, Delta and Echo- has had its special task to complete, and has done so with flying colours. Every individual has risen to the challenge she faced with considerable courage and good nature. It was never easy for them, and often it was desperate as you may hear and read in the weeks and months that follow; but they never gave in, and we, at the base, salute every one of them. **End**

*

Monday 26ᵗʰ May
Internet report

McVitie's Penguin Polar Relay - Update 26 May 1997. More reports:

Penguin Echo have stormed the final 16NM northwards today to reach 90 00N .

Currently at the North Pole awaiting their boarding call. **End**

*

Tuesday 27th May

Victoria:

Having hardly slept all night I was picked up at 7.00am by a taxi to go to the *BBC* studios for a live interview on *BBC Breakfast News*. It was one of the most daunting things that I have ever done. I was so nervous, this was definitely a very different kettle of fish to local radio!! Jan McCormac (Alpha) was also there and while in makeup the producer came up and told us that Echo had made it a few hours previously. From that moment on I had a permanent smile etched on my face, words could not describe the feelings and emotions that were going though my mind. We had made history.

This had not been a life long ambition, but a series of coincidences and being in the right place at the right time, and grasping our opportunities. For Jan and I the day was to become a big blur interspersed with champagne and interviews. *BBC - 6.00pm & 9.00pm, Channel One, London Today/Tonight, ITN 5.40 pm, Daily Telegraph*, all the local papers/radios. The telephone just would not stop. The sad thing is that I never really had a second to myself to come to terms with what had happened.

I have two lasting memories from that day. The first was that finally at the age of twenty six I was actually standing in the Blue Peter Garden. I had been an avid fan as a child, and to film an interview sitting there was just wonderful, the sun was shining and life could not have been more perfect. The other was at the ITN studios, waiting to do an interview for *London Today*. In the waiting area with us were Status Quo, making a comeback after one of them had recovered from a heart attack/operation. To us they were icons, but one of them actually came

214

up and said how amazing he thought we were, especially Mum.

To me this was the biggest lesson I was to learn. For years I had looked up to various explorers and mountaineers such as David Hempleman-Adams and Rebecca Stephens (First British Woman to climb Mount Everest) as role models, and tended to forget that they also led normal lives. Even now people come up to me and say how amazing I am and how brave I must be, and I can never quite understand this, as I see myself as a normal run of the mill person who just happens to have been part of an expedition to the North Pole.

*

Sue:

Lying in bed in France listening to the Today programme and hearing they were about to get to the Pole, a very strange feeling. I felt very far away from them, yet I could still imagine every pace they took and the never ending seascape of frozen ice. When we heard that they had actually arrived, we celebrated in the only way you can in France: a really wonderful lunch, champagne, food very dissimilar to what we had in the Arctic, thank goodness, and excellent wine. A lunch to remember. The next day when returning home on the boat, the newspapers were full of the triumph. I could see everyone reading about it and longed to jump up and say 'I was one of those women and that is my daughter being quoted'!

*

Victoria:

The next day was, surprise surprise, taken up with yet more interviews, *Live TV* and *The Weather Channel*. It was in almost all the papers, which was a huge relief as up till then the coverage of the

215

expedition in the UK had been pretty non-existent. Canada and America had been far more interested in us, which was a sad reflection on the obsession of the British Press with 'bad' news. Here was a positive, feel good story, twenty British women, total amateurs, hoping against all odds to fly the Union Jack at the North Pole, and finally we had the coverage that we deserved.

Slowly but surely it was sinking in, and I started to realise the significance of what had happened - I felt so proud not just of my personal achievement but of the team. In fact not once did I think of it as me, it was always us and this holds true for the rest of the team. Only four of us may have stood at the Pole itself but they could not have got there without the rest of us. It was a team effort.

*

Thursday 29th May
Internet report

McVitie's Penguin Polar Relay - Update 29 May 1997. More reports:

Apologies to all if the enormous success of the expedition has not been matched by the volume of information on the web page. The base camp team all left Resolute on Tuesday to go and pick the triumphant Penguin Echo up from the North Pole. As is the norm it seems with the pick up flights, the weather closed in and the planes have been grounded in Eureka for two days now. So the excitement is not over yet by any means.

This report is being written from the UK base of The Polar Travel

Company deep in the middle of Dartmoor, where the whole event really began in January 1996 at the first selection weekend. Our information is obviously limited since Eureka is even more off the beaten track than Resolute. We have just learnt from the air charter company that as of 17.30 BST the weather is clearing across the Arctic and it is likely that the planes will make the five or six hour flight to the Pole in the near future. No guarantees of course. If this is the case then Penguin Echo should arrive back in the UK on Monday morning. Fingers crossed. I for one will be there.

The phones have been going red hot here from the media *et al* as you might imagine. Everyone seems to believe that we have a hot line to the Pole. We don't. So your guess is as good as ours as to whether Echo actually did run the final miles to the Pole. Their rapid progress suggested as much.

Four hundred and fifteen miles gone and oh yes none to go. **End**

*

Victoria:

By this stage Echo were getting rather fed up and wanted to come home, the elation of standing at the top of the world had quickly worn off, and once they had caught up on their sleep they began to imagine all the celebrations going on without them. We were all waiting with bated breath, when were they going to make it back to England?

Finally they arrived back at Heathrow more than a week after their triumph at the Pole. The atmosphere was impossible to describe and not surprisingly, very emotional. It was all over. What would we do

217

next? Meeting them at the airport, having got up at some ungodly hour, was Dawn French. If ever a patron did her job well, then surely this was it; true dedication to a cause. Speaking to Echo afterwards they have all said that this was one of their lasting memories of their first day back in the UK.

In June the whole team were honoured with an invitation to go to No. 10 to meet the still very new Prime Minister. The day had a rather surreal feel about it as we had to wear our red suits and they looked rather incongruous, especially as it was pouring with rain! We could not have been made to feel more welcome, any question was answered, and we were given a comprehensive guided tour of all the state rooms. A supposed thirty minute visit lasted over an hour. It was fascinating to see round the house, a sort of Tardis like building, tiny from the outside and huge inside. Humphrey, the cat was sitting outside, looking slightly mangy and well past his sell by date. We all took countless photographs, and had a group one with Tony Blair, the Prime Minister. Because of the rain, it was nigh on impossible to find a taxi to take us back to Lucy's flat, so on to the tube it was. In rush hour, in our red suits, we caused quite a stir!

*

Sue:

For me a slightly bizarre occasion. I have done work, not much, but some, with the Conservatives for 30 years, and here I was, a month after the Labour victory, in No 10. I wouldn't have missed it though! Our suits had a sort of lingering smell of the Rookery. Everything that had been there smelt of fuel oil, we didn't notice it particularly when there, more so on our return.

We were still not allowed to tell anyone of our dunking, which was getting ridiculous. They were still saving it for the big story. My answer to interviewers when asked if we got wet is to say that the main wet problem was sweat, which always so surprises them that they forgot they asked about falling in! Lynne and Paula both find having to prevaricate is difficult as well. I think it is too much in the past actually to matter if we tell people in interviews. But it does make an exciting story and was very much part of our leg of the relay.

*

Victoria:

The celebrations continued and a wonderful Polar Party soon followed, Cheryl Baker (ex Bucks Fizz) even appeared in order to film a clip for *Record Breakers*. We were voted Women of the Year, were invited to attend a truly amazing lunch and were mentioned in the Guinness Book of Records, something that every child dreams of!

In the summer I made my second, very painful, big decision. This was something that I had spent many hours thinking about. I had been going out with my boyfriend Jamie on and off for some years and it was obviously getting to the make or break stage. While training he had been an incredible support, calling me on a regular basis from Bosnia where he was based with the army, and once up at Resolute this support continued via letter. Unfortunately so much thinking time can have it's pitfalls and I realised that while I may love Jamie, I was not in love with him. This was an incredibly difficult decision to make and was without a doubt the saddest outcome of the expedition as far as I was concerned.

Overtly therefore my life had changed, both personally and professionally, but had my opinions of the Arctic? I had gone out there expecting a vast white wilderness, but despite having read polar books

219

extensively, nothing could prepare me for what I found. The Arctic is tough, at times it may be terrifying, but it does not have to be life threatening. Getting up in the morning is seriously unpleasant, but life is like that when you are working. The food is boring, but you get bored with normal food anyway. The hardships which the media pick up, the cold and lack of comforts, are not really an issue, instead it is the unknown that causes fear.

Even the unknown has a certain quality about it. The landscape changes constantly, and I felt as if I was watching evolution first hand. What was flat one minute, suddenly had been replaced by a twenty foot ridge. An incredibly powerful place which is definitely not hostile, I felt very welcome and incredibly at ease and I never once felt lonely. On our return a hot bath had been the main priority, but I was surprised to find that I had not missed material things such as food and wine. Britain itself I missed: have you ever noticed how many shades of green there are, and how many different cloud formations? Coming back to day and night was very weird, and noises are far more acute now.

I have been incredibly lucky to experience a place where very few people will ever go. I for one will certainly be returning.

*

Sue:

Since coming back I have discovered enormous confidence, and I think the whole team feels the same. We know if something is possible we can do it. The person who has found it the hardest is Jeremy. Dave Hempleman-Adams said that the one left at home is the one to find it difficult to cope with the changed partner. The partner who has been away is on a high and wants to talk nonstop, the one left at home gets fed

220

up and bored after a few days. Absolutely everyone wanted to ask about it, and it became embarrassing sometimes as we tried to change the subject and no one wanted to. Victoria and I are definitely closer, and it is wonderful to have someone to talk to about our expedition for the rest of my life. It is important to remember when part of an expedition such as this, that despite the incredible sense of teamwork and friendship it is almost impossible to be one hundred per cent honest with each other, particularly when things are not going according to plan and morale is low. However, when going with your daughter this is not a problem. We could both say what we really felt, deep down; we may have fallen out or disagreed at times, but ultimately the falling out never lasted for long.

I think that life, and the appreciation of it, has become more important. Small things have been put into perspective, and I think we have become more laid back about trivial matters such as traffic jams. I definitely appreciate life more, though the time in hospital helped that. One thing we learned was that deprivation is good for appreciation. I find that I have now an awareness of being happy most of the time, an 'isn't life just wonderful' sort of feeling.

It will never be possible to describe adequately the amazing sights and sounds we have seen and heard, until you have been there you can't really imagine it. It was unlike anything I had imagined, this strange world of moving ice - though you rarely see the movement, only your instruments tell you. People ask us, were we upset at not being members of the final team? Our answer is that they wouldn't have got there without us doing our leg; and who knows, the lump of ice we camped on one night may well have been the North Pole a month or two earlier. It isn't like the South Pole, with a marker that stays in place, it is just a mass of moving ice in the winter, and in the summer a wave or ripple in the sea becomes the pole for a fraction of a second. The Arctic is an astoundingly clean place, no pollution, no smells, your hair and clothes remain clean, you come across no man made rubbish, and as a result your other senses are intensified.

The marvellous quality of the Arctic is that you are there with five other people from whom you cannot escape, all of whom you can see every second of the day, yet when you walk you are in a capsule of private thought. To have had nearly six weeks of prime thinking time is a privilege, almost like being in retreat! When at home this same capsule can be recreated when I walk with my dogs, but it is never quite the same quality thinking time, there always seem to be distractions. Everyone needs space and a chance to just think.

One of the greatest differences between our all women expedition and men's expeditions is the way we go about getting to the Pole. Men like to conquer, fight, or subdue the Arctic, while we, I believe, had a different attitude. We felt that we had to go along with what we were faced with, we 'went with the flow'. We tried to have the Arctic on our side instead of confronting it. Instead of feeling that we had to climb the vast pressure ridge in front of us, we looked for an easier way round, which meant that perhaps our sledges became less damaged. We knew that our physical strength would not be the ultimate force, but our willingness to compromise, to find a less strenuous solution to any problem. Perhaps this meant that we might walk a little further, but in the end our strength was conserved.

As women we are used to accepting what is thrown at us and surviving, so problems like falling in become part of the routine day to

222

day problems that have to be coped with. You find a way to dry your clothes, and in the end, all turns out well. Pen Hadow was right when he said that there was no reason women could not get to the Pole, and he was right when he suggested that it would be done in a very different way, the softly, softly approach.

Now I find I have a confidence, not cockiness I hope, but a feeling that I can achieve. I would never have thought that I would be giving talks, let alone motivational ones! But I do feel that I have something to say, and by saying *what* I feel somehow firms up *how* I feel myself. The sort of things that are important for people to understand in order to develop their full potential are so simple, but until you put them into words you don't actually realise that the awareness of these thoughts is important.

As I talk mainly to women I obviously concentrate on how they can develop in a man's world. For example, women are brought up to consider themselves as carers, which indeed they are when they have a family at home, but once the children have left they should not have guilty feelings when they want to achieve something for themselves, even though others think that they may be selfish.

'Own time' is very important. You should always look to the future and have goals in front of you, however small, and you must recognise opportunities and grab them. Because if *you* don't, someone else will and will have the chance that you missed! It's much better to say yes and think about how you will carry it out afterwards. You can usually find the way round a problem

The fact that I had cancer has had a huge influence on how I feel now, how I felt when the expedition was first mooted, and how I reacted to the event as a whole. If you have had cancer, life means a lot more. You experience a great contrast in feelings. First of all, your worries change, the day to day ones don't seem to exist in the same way. Strangely enough, for me, most worries have disappeared. You actually seem to be much more able to take each day as it comes. This doesn't mean to say that you are not frightened of the future, but the future, I feel, will look after itself. I would hate to know what the future holds.

To me one of the great joys of life is the unexpected, the luck of being in the right time at the right place, as in the fact that Victoria saw about the expedition in the paper. Or, you could say, we were there in the right time at the right place after we had fallen in, and the ice moved to help us get to the other side. I feel that for me the expedition has drawn a line under having had cancer, it is finished. But now I would like to be able to talk about cancer to those who have gone through, or are about to go through, the same experience, because just talking can be a great comfort and allay worries. I can tell those who have been diagnosed that having breast cancer need not stop you doing anything, and that having a positive attitude can help in the healing process.

I do find one of the hardest things to cope with now is the fact that everyone thinks you have been incredibly brave, but in reality one had no choice, it was literally sink or swim! We show our photographs and people can't believe that we pulled our sledges over ridges, or survived living in the cold, but when you are out there doing it the day to day Arctic existence becomes the norm. We weren't frightened at the time of falling in, human beings are great survivors, and as our bodies were hot when we went down we could keep going, but it was the next day that was so bad.

I don't think I have ever been so frightened in my life, a dry mouth, heart beating madly and a stomach that felt as if a stone was in it. But by the next evening we were already feeling that if we had survived so far we would certainly survive the rest! I keep saying that anyone with a modicum of fitness could have succeeded in being selected, though of course the bottom line is whether you have the will to do it. But it is still rather embarrassing when you are told that you are brave, because neither of us feel that we have been *that* special. Perhaps we coped because we are both rather bossy, quite strong women! But we certainly aren't superwomen.

The Arctic certainly has not let itself become forgotten in the past six months. There have been endless talks, and I have discovered a whole new career for myself in public speaking, something else that has come out of the expedition. So far I have had only one question I could not answer: 'how far was it from Wolverhampton to the North Pole?' This was from a child in a primary school! Another child at the same school asked me a question that keeps cropping up amongst small children, 'did I meet Father Christmas?' I just say he was resting after a busy Christmas!

Looking back to our expedition everything seems to be still this dreamworld. You are not on land, but are walking and camping; you are on the ocean, but you are not in a boat, or swimming (or at least, not much!). There is never a fixed point in your world, apart from the imaginary geographical point of the North Pole itself, but you can't see that. It is not a real place. The last team actually arrived at the Pole, were there for several hours, then their own particular, private, North Pole drifted south, the only way it could go, towards Russia. When they were eventually picked up they had travelled nearly 16 miles, still on their own Pole!

It was the longest three weeks of my life, not because it was so terrible, but because of the timelessness of the whole place. Watches, apart from being useful in telling you which way to go, were for me very unimportant. The only time that you felt time dragging was sometimes in the last hour of walking, when your body began to tell you it was time to have a rest. It was long because you had no natural breaks at the end of the day, with night falling to divide one day from the next. So you went to sleep in sunlight, and woke up to the same. It was long in that each day was the same, yet this didn't matter, they ran into each other, and towards the end we actually began to feel we didn't know the day or the hour! It was long because you were trying to savour every second of this amazing experience, with the thought that the chances of ever returning were very unlikely, so you had to put every second of experience into your head. You were terrified of missing something and, despite there being a lack of variety in the types of colours, you still looked at every lump of ice as if you had never seen ice before.

But something that has been very difficult to explain to people without them actually having seen photographs, is the non-whiteness of the Arctic. It is every imaginable graduation of shades of white through blue to lilac, to the black of the sea, with the sun creating incredible effects. The one thing you never have is pure whiteness. Perhaps because we were all totally unused to the Arctic we took a certain naive pleasure each day in just being there, and, perhaps, just 'being'. Finally, it was long because you couldn't let a second's worth of experience escape, so your whole body became immersed in the feel of the Arctic,

226

ultimately you became part of the Arctic, your body somehow adapted itself to this strange life and felt as if it had been there for ever.

Would I have taken part in this expedition if the chance had arisen at some other time in my life? I don't really know, it is very hard to answer any 'what if' question truthfully, because circumstances change and responsibilities are different. I was very lucky that everything - my children leaving home, my catering business finishing, and a sort of mid life turning point -all came at the same time as the expedition. So if there was any time in my life to have the opportunity to do something totally mad and perhaps in retrospect irresponsible, this was it.

I say irresponsible because Jeremy *was* worried, as also were my parents. I think that my father actually became rather unwell as a result, but I am afraid to say I still don't regret for an instant having said 'yes' to Victoria in August 1995. There has to be one glorious time in everyone's life when you say 'to hell with responsibilities and everyone else, I am going to do what I want'! My one problem is that travel, talking and writing have become addictive, so where do I go from here? The Antarctic perhaps, where I can see penguins that I won't want to eat, where I would see the Southern Cross and experience ice that doesn't move!

The Arctic is an ephemeral place. What you are seeing and walking on may not be there in two months time. Nothing lasts. You forget that it is not land, and that it is constantly changing. In a way the Arctic is analogous with life. You can't change what you've been past, you don't know what's ahead, and even the present is entirely unpredictable. And when you are no longer there, the kind of limbo you were living in does not exist. It has melted away as if it had never been there.

227

Postscript

Victoria:

Since we wrote this book, I have indeed gone back to the Arctic. Lucy Roberts, who was on the final leg, and myself are intending to become the first British Women to walk the whole way to the North Pole in 1999. We have spent the last eight months planning the expedition and I am writing this within days of our return from a training expedition up at Resolute Bay. To revisit Resolute was one of the most wonderful times of my life. It is one of those places where life seems to stand still - the scenery, the people, even the gossip, nothing has changed.

I was very concerned that I wanted to return for all the wrong reasons, the most terrifying experience can look rosy in retrospect, and I have to admit to enjoying the attention that goes with being part of a successful polar expedition.

However, even after spending five days snow bound in a tent during appalling storms I was still able to say that I was 'enjoying' myself and only then did I know that I was there for the right reasons. I feel so at home whilst in the Arctic, the beauty and serenity are indescribable. My friends and family will back me up when I say that I am a fairly talkative person, however this is the one place on earth where I am happy to be totally silent.

I am fully aware of the dangers and unpredictability that we will face next year, but returning this year has finally put to rest my fear of open water. The only way forward now is North.

breakthrough
breast cancer

Dear Reader,

I am pleased to inform you that by buying this book you have contributed to the work of Breakthrough Breast Cancer.

Breakthrough Breast Cancer is a charity committed to funding research to discover what causes breast cancer - how it can be prevented, and to develop new treatments so that ultimately the disease can be eradicated.

Together with the Institute of Cancer Breakthrough is opening the first centre in the UK wholly dedicated to breast cancer research - The Toby Robins Breast Cancer Research Centre which will bring together leading scientists to focus on the disease.

Breakthrough is supported by thousands of people - groups or individuals - who have taken up the Breakthrough £1,000 Challenge to raise that sum for the charity. Between them, they have raised over £4 million. Sue and Victoria are an inspiration to us all and show that with determination we can achieve great things.

If you would like to hear more about Breakthrough's work or to make a donation please write to us at Breakthrough Breast Cancer, PO Box 7012, London, E1 8AZ or call us on 0171 405 5111.

Best Wishes,

Delyth Morgan
<u>Chief Executive</u>

10 pence from the sale of each copy of Frigid Women will go to BEL which covenants all its taxible profits to Breakthrough Breast Cancer, (a registered charity, number .1062636)

Appendix 1.

Food

These are the figures for the food for the entire expedition. This should provide enough for:

1. 6 people x 10 weeks on the ice, man-hauling.
2. Back-up team, 3 people, at base camp in Resolute Bay for the duration of the trip.
3. Each team in training at base camp before going onto the ice, as well as the returning teams who have just finished their leg.

Porridge oats 120 kg	Powdered milk 45 kg	Salami 150 kg
Crackers 30 kg	Chocolate 100 kg	Peanuts 35 kg
Cashews/almonds 35 kg	Nuts and raisins 30 kg	Dried apricots & figs 50 kg
Dried raisins 25 kg	Muesli bars 75 kg	Energy bars 30 kg
Noodles 35 kg	Dried soup 20 kg	Dried Cheese 50 kg
Hot chocolate 50 kg	Tea 15 kg	Energy drink crystals 85 kg
Sugar 20 kg	Penguin biscuits- 7000!	

In the end what we actually took with us, for each individual person per day was;

Breakfast - Cereal, with added raisins and milk powder.

Drinks - Tea, coffee, hot chocolate and sugar lumps.

Snacks - Mixed fruit and nuts, approx. eight slices of salami, parma ham or pancetta, ten squares of chocolate, a muesli bar, six penguin biscuits and fruit crystals dissolved in our water bottles.

Dinner - Chicken noodle soup, 4 lumps of cheese, nearly half a pound of butter per person, pasta and two pieces of shortbread, plus drinks.

In total - approx. 6000 calories a day per person. Not wildly gastronomic, but very sustaining, none of us lost or gained weight during our walking time.

Appendix 2.

ARGOS Codes

0	Conditions OK, going well
1	Conditions poor, slow going
2	Halted by bad weather, bad ice or open water
3.	Radio out of commission, no further radio comms possible
4.	Weather poor, resupply/change over not possible
5.	Overcast, visibility good, strip marked, land on lead
6.	Overcast, visibility good, strip marked, land on multi year ice
7.	Conditions changed, delay flight, await instructions
8.	Conditions excellent, good for change over
9.	Resupply needed ASAP
10.	Need medic on evacuation plane, await further instructions
11.	Need to evacuate a guide, not urgent
12.	Need to evacuate a guide, ASAP
13.	Need to evacuate four or less people, not urgent
14.	Need to evacuate four or less people, ASAP
15.	Need to evacuate whole group, ASAP
16.	SOS - every button is pressed.

Numbers 0-3 were for general information, not to be acted on

Numbers 4-8 were for the pilots information

Numbers 8-15 were requests for changeover, resupply or evacuation

If the emergency code was used, ARGOS, in Maryland would phone First Air, (the pilots who flew us on and off the ice).

If two consecutive transmissions were not received then a search and rescue mission would be called out.

Appendix 3.

Polar Traffic

There were seven expeditions on the ice:

1. McVities Penguin Polar Relay (British)

2. British Typhoo - Britain and Norway have been expedition rivals for almost 100 yrs since Scott was beaten to the South Pole by Amundsen - However this was David Hempleman-Adams 40 yrs (Britain) and Rune Gjeldnes 25 yrs (Norway) - An unsupported expedition, reportedly the first joint British/Norwegian expedition to the North Pole.

3. Polar Free - Self Sufficient Human Powered Expedition - Nobu Narita 29 yrs (Japan), Acchan Niyhahwa 30 yrs (Japan) and David Scott 29 yrs (New Zealand). It was named for its environmental commitment to leave no trace behind. They promised that all traces of the expedition would be eaten, burnt or taken out at the end.

4. Hyoichi Kohno 39 yrs (Japan) - resupplied expedition to the North Pole.

5. Dutch x 5 - a supported expedition to the North Pole. The team had previously been on expeditions to Mount Everest and K2.

6. Alan Bywater (British/Canadian) - failed.

7. Pam Flowers 50yrs - Solo attempt to the North Pole, failed at an early stage.

There were also various Magnetic North Pole expeditions.

There was one man Kayaking to the North Pole from the other side.

Appendix 4.

General Kit

The kit that we had with us throughout the expedition (see Appendix 5. for clothing and personal kit):

Throw Bag	Shovel	Climbing Rope
Ice Screws	Pulleys	Ice Axe
MSR Stoves x 4	Snow Brush	EPERB - Emergency Beacon
Team Diary	Hacksaw	GPS
Signal Mirror	Rifle	

4 litres fuel per day, 2 for heating and 2 for cooking

Appendix 5

Personal Items

Washing kit	Toothpaste (one tube between us all)
Toothbrush	Flannel
Tiny bit of soap	Shared deodorant
Face cream	Medication
Basic First Aid	Tampax
One book each	Our diary
Pencils	Goggles
Tissues	Wet Wipes.
Dark glasses	

Sue - Lapsang teabags   Victoria - banoffi mixture

Spare clothing - The only spares we took were a change of thin socks, a change of thick socks, spare gloves, windproof trousers, windproof jacket and a spare neck gaiter. The guides had one set of spare boot liners, but no spare skiis or poles.

The guides carried any remaining items such as the tent, radio etc.

Appendix 6.

<u>Chart showing daily progress</u>

McVitie's Penguin Polar Relay - Charlie Team

Day	Date	Position PM	Temp PM ^{0}C	Position Next AM	Temp Next AM - ^{0}C	Miles Day/Total
1	11/04	85'10,74'25	-26	85'09,74'16	-24	00/00
2	12/04	85'16,73'24	-24	85'17,73'08	-24	06/06
3	13/04	85'23,73'25	-24	85'24,73'24	-30	07/13
4	14/04	85'30,73'37	-28	85'30,73'39	-27	07/20
5	15/04	85'36,73'52	-25	85'36,73'40	-24	06/26
6	16/04	85'45,73'46	-22	85'45,73'42	-24	09/35
7	17/04	85'54,73'51	-25	85'55,73'37	-18	09/44
8	18/04	86'02,73'42	-27	86'02,73'05	-27	08/52
9	19/04	86'06,72'02	-23	86'06,69'46	-20	04/56
10	20/04	86'06,68'42	-20	86'07,67'44	-19	00/56
11	21/04	86'10,67'59	-20	86'09,67'17	-20	04/60
12	22/04	86'12,67'00	-18	86'12,66'22	-19	02/62
13	23/04	86'18,66'01	-15	86'16,65'09	-12	06/68
14	24/04	86'18,64'39	-12	86'16,63'24	-15	00/68
15	25/04	86'14,62'23	-17	86'13,61'53	-15	00/68
16	26/04	86'18,61'42	-15	86'18,61'28	-14	04/68
17	27/04	86'21,61'19	-14	86'21,61'18	-15	03/71

Other Titles from
Travellerseye

A Trail of Visions
Route 1: India, Sri Lanka, Thailand, Sumatra.

Photographer & Author	Vicki Couchman
Editor	Dan Hiscocks
ISBN 1 871349 33 8	R.R.P. £14.99

"A Trail of Visions tells with clarity what it is like to follow a trail, both the places you see and the people you meet."

Independent on Sunday

Route 2: Peru, Bolivia, Ecuador, Columbia.

Photographer & Author	Vicki Couchman
Editor	Dan Hiscocks
ISBN 0 953 0575 0X	R.R.P. £16.99

"The illustrated guide"

The Times

Travellers Tales from Heaven & Hell

Author	Various
Editor	Dan Hiscocks
ISBN 0 953 0575 18	R.R.P. £6.99

An eclectic collection of annecdotal travel stories - the best from thousands of competition entries. "...an inpirational experience. I couldn't wait to leave the country and encounter the next inevitable disaster".

Simon Calder Presenter BBC Travel Show

Discovery Road

Authors	Tim Garratt & Andy Brown
Editor	Dan Hiscocks
ISBN 0 953 0575 34	R.R.P. £7.99

"We are taken on a voyage of self discovery and are confronted with some of the crucial issues facing everyone living in the world today. Readers will surely find themselves reassessing their lives and be inspired to reach out and follow their own dreams."

Sir Ranulph Fiennes Explorer